Nonfiction Reading Comprehension: Grades 5-6

Authors: Schyrlet Cameron and Suzanne Myers
Editors: Mary Dieterich and Sarah M. Anderson
Proofreader: Margaret Brown

ISBN 978-1-58037-615-0

Printing No. CD-404166

Mark Twain Media, Inc., Publishers
Distributed by Carson-Dellosa Publishing LLC

Visit us at www.carsondellosa.com

Table of Contents

Introduction to the Teacher

The ability to comprehend nonfiction is critical for student success on standardized tests. The classroom reading experience is top-heavy with fiction. This limits the student's practice in reading nonfiction. The majority of selections in most basal/reading series are literary/narrative text. In the past few years, there has been an increase in nonfiction text being included within basal readers; however, the amount is still disproportionate. *Nonfiction Reading Comprehension: Grades 5–6* will provide students in grades 5 and 6 practice in reading nonfiction selections and testing for comprehension.

This book contains nonfiction reading selections covering a variety of content areas: science, history, geography, economics, and informational text. Each content area includes one short passage, four reading selections, and one set of paired passages. The short passage is intended to be teacher-directed. This will allow the teacher to introduce, model, or review reading strategies and how to apply them to test-taking. The four student reading selections provide independent student practice. The paired passages require students to compare/contrast two reading passages on similar topics.

The Flesch-Kincaid Readability Scale was used to determine the readability level of the reading selections, which range from a 5.0 to 6.9 reading level. The five student reading selections in each content area are arranged from the lowest to highest reading level.

Reading selections are followed by a page of comprehension questions written in standardized-test format—fill in the bubble for multiple choice and write a constructed response. A variety of questioning strategies were used in the development of the multiple-choice questions. The constructed response questions require students to support their answers with details. The questions cover the most tested reading comprehension skills, such as locate information, determine the meaning of words or phrases, identify the main idea, draw inferences, and compare/contrast. This method will help students become familiar with the testing process, which will reduce test anxiety. This will result in improved standardized test scores.

SHORT PASSAGE SCIENCE

Earthquakes

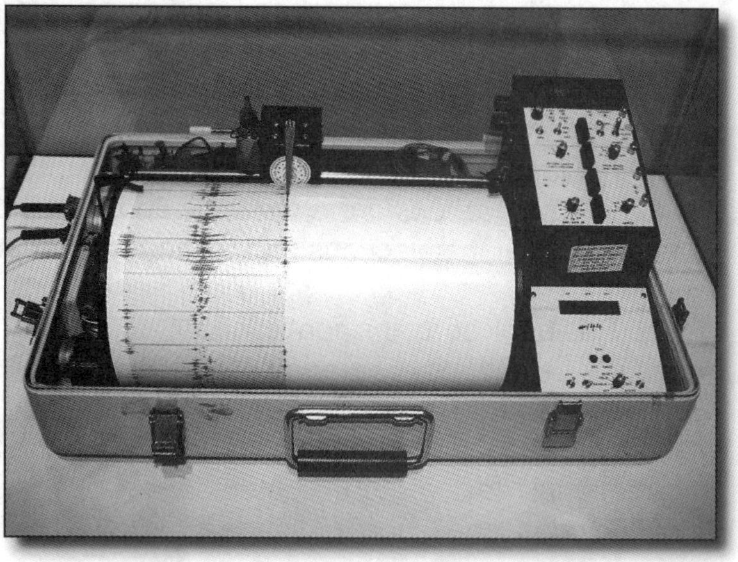

The shaking, trembling, or rolling movements usually caused by bodies of rock slipping past each other at faults are called earthquakes. The point beneath the earth where the rocks move is called the focus of a quake. The epicenter is the spot directly above the focus on the earth's surface.

Seismographs record earthquake waves. The machine has a pen suspended on a weighted wire that hangs above a rotating drum of paper. When the earth moves, the drum moves, and the pen traces a spike. The height of the tallest spike is used to measure the strength of a quake on the Richter scale. Quakes fall within a range of 1 to 10 on this scale.

Earthquakes can cause damage by bringing buildings and bridges down, destroying highways, and breaking gas lines. They can also cause huge ocean waves called tsunamis. About one million earthquakes occur annually, but most go unnoticed. A few hundred of these make major changes to the earth's surface. A dozen or so cause severe damage and loss of human life.

Name: ______________________ Date: ______________________

Earthquakes

Directions: Fill in the bubble next to the correct answer for each multiple-choice question.

1. The purpose of the second paragraph of the passage is to
   - ◯ a. identify the stages of an earthquake.
   - ◯ b. explain how an earthquake happens.
   - ◯ c. describe the damage caused by an earthquake.
   - ◯ d. tell how a seismograph works.

2. Which word is a synonym for the word <u>annually</u> as it is used in the passage?
   - ◯ a. daily
   - ◯ b. monthly
   - ◯ c. yearly
   - ◯ d. centennially

3. Most earthquakes
   - ◯ a. go unnoticed.
   - ◯ b. produce severe damage.
   - ◯ c. make major changes on the earth's surface.
   - ◯ d. cause the loss of human life.

4. The picture helps you to understand how
   - ◯ a. a Richter scale works.
   - ◯ b. to locate the epicenter of an earthquake.
   - ◯ c. a seismograph works.
   - ◯ d. an earthquake can change the earth's surface.

5. Explain why it is important to have laws for the construction of buildings in areas with frequent earthquake activity. Use details from the passage to support your answer.

____

____

____

____

____

____

Amphibians

Amphibians are a class of vertebrates. Vertebrates are animals that have a backbone. Amphibians are cold-blooded, just like fish and reptiles. They cannot produce their own body heat. If the temperature around them is cold, the amphibian becomes cold and lazy. Its body functions slow down.

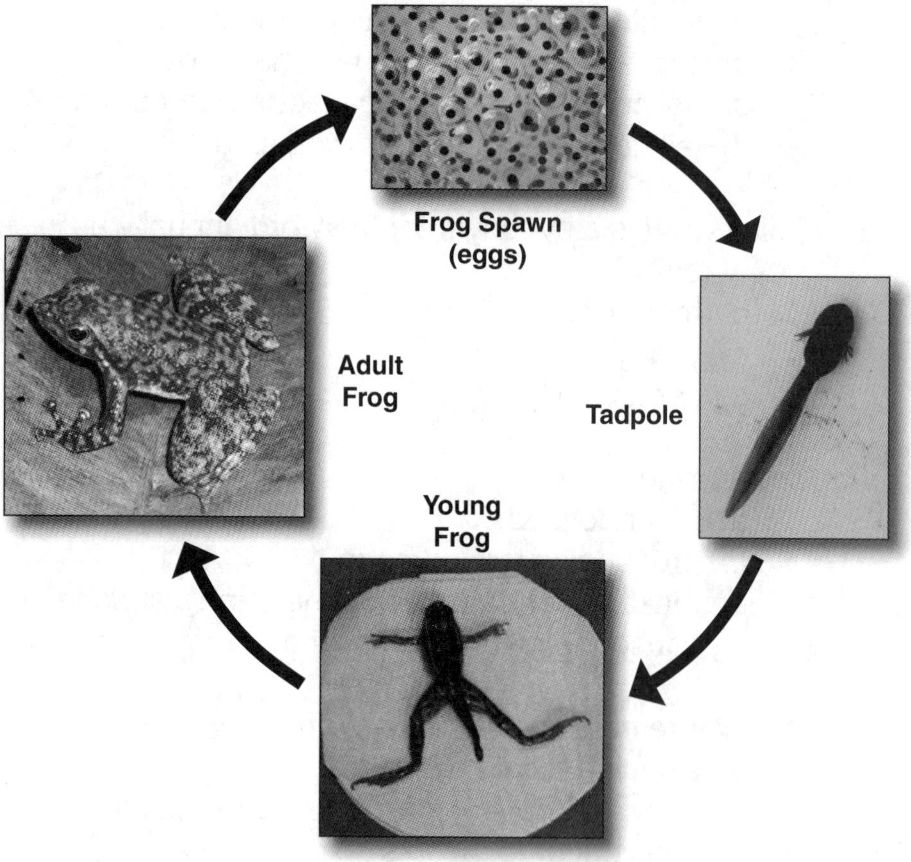

The name amphibian means "double life." This refers to the fact that they live part of their lives in water and part of their lives on land. For example, frogs go through a life cycle called <u>metamorphosis</u>: a change from egg to tadpole to adult frog. Tadpoles have gills and must live in water. Adult frogs have lungs and can live on land.

The skin of most amphibians is soft and moist. Toads, however, have dry, rough skin covered with bumps that look like warts. Amphibians usually feel sticky to the touch. Glands in the skin produce a thick, slimy substance called mucus. This keeps the skin moist, and it keeps the skin from drying out. Some amphibians have special glands, called parotid glands, that secrete a poisonous substance. This helps to repel their enemies.

Amphibians must return to water to mate and lay their eggs. Amphibian eggs are called spawn. The spawn do not have a shell and would dry out if they were laid on land. The females of most toad and frog species lay hundreds of eggs at once. Frog spawn is laid in one big mass. Toad spawn is laid in long strings. Other female amphibians lay their eggs one at a time beside underwater plants.

There are about 3,000 different species of amphibians. Living amphibians are divided into three groups based on their body structures: frogs and toads; salamanders, sirens, and newts; and the odd caecilians.

COMPREHENSION TEST SCIENCE

Name: ______________________ Date: ______________________

Amphibians

Directions: Fill in the bubble next to the correct answer for each multiple-choice question.

1. What is another possible title for this selection?
   - ○ a. Life Cycle of a Frog
   - ○ b. Characteristics of Amphibians
   - ○ c. Toads and Frogs
   - ○ d. Vertebrates

2. What words or phrase from the selection help define the word metamorphosis?
   - ○ a. double life
   - ○ b. cold-blooded
   - ○ c. a change
   - ○ d. special glands

3. All amphibians lay their eggs in
   - ○ a. water.
   - ○ b. sand.
   - ○ c. soil.
   - ○ d. mud.

4. Amphibians are divided into three groups based on
   - ○ a. type of skin.
   - ○ b. laying of eggs.
   - ○ c. life cycle.
   - ○ d. body structure.

5. Describe how being cold-blooded affects the life of an amphibian. Use details from the selection to support your answer.

____

____

____

____

____

____

READING SELECTION 2 SCIENCE

Magnets

A magnet is a device that attracts certain metals, such as iron, nickel, and cobalt. It can also attract or repel another magnet. The first magnets used by people were lodestones. Lodestone, an iron ore, is called magnetite. It is found naturally in the earth's surface and has unique magnetic qualities. People would carry a piece of lodestone on a string. The free-hanging magnet would point north. If they knew which direction was north, then it was easy to locate east, west, and south.

Magnets come in a variety of sizes, shapes, and strengths. Two of the most common types are the bar and horseshoe magnets. No matter what the shape is, the magnet will have two poles, or ends. One pole is a north pole; and the other is a south pole.

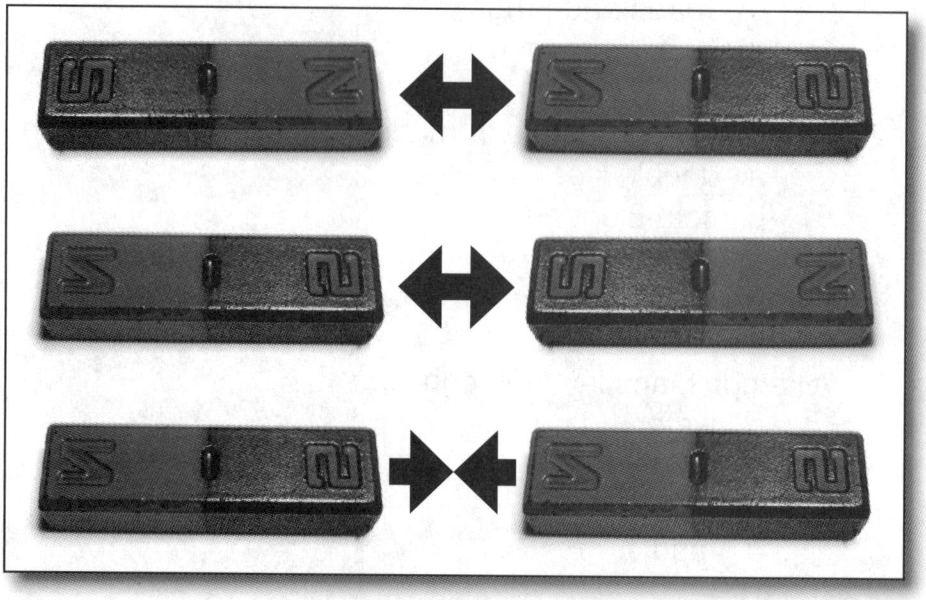

Magnetic force is the attractive or repulsive force between the poles of magnets. If two magnets are placed near each other, the north pole of one will attract the south pole of the other. If you place north poles toward each other, they will repel each other. If you place south poles toward each other, they will repel each other. Remember: like poles repel and unlike poles attract each other.

There are permanent magnets and temporary magnets. A permanent magnet is one that will hold its magnetic properties over a long period of time. Magnetite is a permanent magnet. Most permanent magnets we use are manufactured. They are a combination, or alloy, of iron, nickel, and cobalt. A temporary magnet is one that will lose its magnetism. A magnet can be used to make a temporary magnet out of other metals. You must take the magnet and stroke the metal piece a few times in one direction.

Be sure to handle a magnet with care. Magnets can lose their magnetic properties. A magnet can be destroyed if it is hit hard, dropped, or heated. Never store magnets with other magnets or metal objects. Magnets should never come in contact with items like credit cards or computers. When handled correctly, magnets are useful tools.

COMPREHENSION TEST **SCIENCE**

Name: ______________________ Date: ______________________

Magnets

Directions: Fill in the bubble next to the correct answer for each multiple-choice question.

1. What is the main idea of paragraph four?
   - ○ a. Magnets are a combination of iron, nickel, and cobalt.
   - ○ b. All magnets are manufactured.
   - ○ c. There are differences between permanent and temporary magnets.
   - ○ d. Magnets come in a variety of sizes, shapes, and strengths.

2. What is an antonym for the word **repel**?
   - ○ a. resist
   - ○ b. attract
   - ○ c. move
   - ○ d. force

3. The first magnets used by people were
   - ○ a. lodestones.
   - ○ b. bar magnets.
   - ○ c. temporary magnets.
   - ○ d. devices.

4. In this selection, what is the purpose of the illustration?
   - ○ a. to show like poles repel and unlike poles attract each other
   - ○ b. to show magnets have a north and south pole
   - ○ c. to show the poles of magnets are labeled
   - ○ d. to show properties of permanent and temporary magnets

5. Explain the difference between a permanent and temporary magnet. Use details from the selection to support your answer.

____

____

____

____

____

____

READING SELECTION 3 **SCIENCE**

Electricity

A turbine (left) turns a generator (right) to produce electricity.

Electricity is an important power source. It is used to produce light and heat and to run motors. We get it by converting natural resources, such as coal, natural gas, or wind, into energy. These resources are called primary sources of energy.

A primary source of energy powers a turbine. The turbine runs a generator. The generator turns large copper coils inside huge magnets. This produces electricity. A transformer sends the electric current to the power lines. The electricity is carried to the user through wires.

Everything is made of matter. Matter is made up of tiny parts called atoms. Each atom has three even tinier parts. These parts are protons, electrons, and neutrons. The nucleus is the center of the atom.

Electricity is made from the movement of electrons. The protons and electrons of an atom are attracted to each other. They both carry an electrical charge. Protons have a positive charge (+). Electrons have a negative charge (-). When an atom is in balance, it has an equal number of protons and electrons. When atoms are not balanced, they need to gain an electron. Electrons can be made to move from one atom to another. A proton that has a positive charge attracts an electron that has a negative charge. When an electron moves between atoms, a current of electricity is created. As one electron is attached to an atom and another electron is lost, it creates a flow of electrons.

Electricity is measured in units called watts. One watt is a very small amount of power. A kilowatt represents 1,000 watts. A kilowatt-hour (kWh) is equal to the energy of 1,000 watts working for one hour. The amount of electricity is measured in kilowatt-hours. The amount charged for each kilowatt-hour is called the rate.

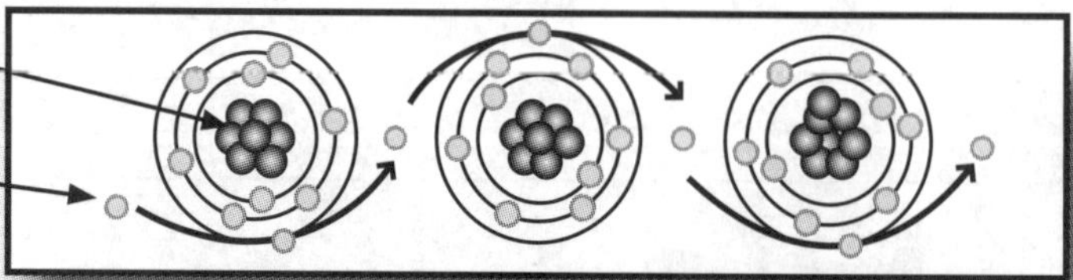

Name: ______________________ Date: ______________________

Electricity

Directions: Fill in the bubble next to the correct answer for each multiple-choice question.

1. The author most likely wrote this passage in order
   - ○ a. to inform.
   - ○ b. to persuade.
   - ○ c. to entertain.
   - ○ d. to convince.

2. They are in **orbit** like the planets around the sun.
   What definition of **orbit** is used in the sentence above?
   - ○ a. spin
   - ○ b. rotate
   - ○ c. path
   - ○ d. circle

3. What units are used to measure electricity?
   - ○ a. rate
   - ○ b. electrons
   - ○ c. hours
   - ○ d. watts

4. Electricity is made from the movement of
   - ○ a. protons.
   - ○ b. electrons.
   - ○ c. neutrons.
   - ○ d. atoms.

5. Explain how coal is used to produce electricity. Use details from the selection to support your answer.

____

____

____

____

____

____

READING SELECTION 4 **SCIENCE**

The Milky Way

Stars are clustered in groups called galaxies. Galaxies can contain billions or even hundreds of billions of stars. Some of them are giant spirals, some of them are shaped like ellipses, and others are irregular in shape.

A view of the core of the Milky Way

We live in a large spiral galaxy called the Milky Way. If we could see it from far out in space, it would look something like a pinwheel. Our galaxy is about 100,000 light years in diameter. Most of its outer region is a flattened spiral of stars called the galactic disk. The stars in the disk are organized into three or four spiral trails, called arms. The arms wind outward from the center. The sun is between 25,000 and 30,000 light years from the center of the galaxy along one of these spiral arms. The disk is relatively thin. It is only about 2,000 light years thick. The center of the galaxy is filled by a large sphere of closely packed stars. They are called the central bulge. It is about 25,000 light years in diameter.

The Milky Way is home to a huge number of stars, about 100 billion. Its mass is about 200 billion times the mass of the sun. These numbers are so large that they are almost hard to imagine. The galaxy also contains vast clouds of dust and gas. The dust clouds make it difficult for us to see the long distance through the galactic disk and the central bulge.

The Milky Way is an example of a spiral galaxy.

Our galaxy is surrounded by a spherical cloud of more than 200 clusters of stars. The cloud is called the halo. The clusters of stars are known as globular clusters. The globular clusters are around 30 to 100 light years in diameter. Each cluster contains 100,000 to 1,000,000 stars.

When we look at the sky at night, we see the Milky Way as a whitish-gray swath across the heavens. This is our view from Earth of the galactic disk and the central bulge. We only see a part of these because much of our view is obscured by dust clouds. If we look in the direction of the constellation Sagittarius, we are looking toward the center of the galaxy. If we look toward Perseus, we are looking at the edge of the galactic disk.

Comprehension Test **Science**

Name: ______________________ Date: ______________________

The Milky Way

Directions: Fill in the bubble next to the correct answer for each multiple-choice question.

1. This selection is **mostly** about
   - ◯ a. what the Milky Way looks like from Earth.
   - ◯ b. the shape of the galactic disk.
   - ◯ c. the characteristics of the Milky Way galaxy.
   - ◯ d. the clouds of dust and gas in the Milky Way galaxy.

2. In the last paragraph, the word **obscured** means
   - ◯ a. surrounded.
   - ◯ b. improved.
   - ◯ c. highlighted.
   - ◯ d. hidden.

3. The diameter of the Milky Way is
   - ◯ a. 100,000 kilometers.
   - ◯ b. 100,000 light years.
   - ◯ c. 1,000,000 stars.
   - ◯ d. 30–100 light years.

4. In the selection, the caption beneath the illustration helps the readers to understand
   - ◯ a. that the color of outer space is black.
   - ◯ b. that the color of stars is yellow.
   - ◯ c. the shape of a spiral galaxy.
   - ◯ d. the sun is at the center of the galaxy.

5. Describe what the Milky Way would look like from space. Use details from the selection to support your answer.

____

____

____

____

____

____

PAIRED PASSAGES SCIENCE

Animal Kingdom

Passage One: Invertebrates

An invertebrate is an animal that does not have a backbone. They make up 95 percent of all known animals. They can be found almost anywhere on the earth: forests, deserts, caves, or oceans.

Scientists have already given names to over one million species of invertebrates. This group includes sponges, worms, mollusk, and arthropods. Most of these are small and slow-moving.

Some of these animals travel around while others do not. Crabs and insects move around their entire lives. Sponges move from place to place when they are very young. An adult sponge will attach to a hard surface such as a rock. It will stay there for the rest of its life.

Invertebrates have an exoskeleton or no skeleton at all. The exoskeleton protects and supports the animal's body. It is made of a hard, waterproof substance called chitin. Some of these animals must shed the exoskeleton in order to grow and reach adulthood.

Passage Two: Vertebrates

A vertebrate is an animal that has a backbone. A backbone consists of a spinal column and a cranium. Only five percent of the known species of animals are vertebrates. They are the most complex organisms in the animal kingdom.

Most vertebrates have very advanced nervous systems. They have muscles and skeletons. They have a highly developed brain enclosed by a skull. They are smart and can move about. This group of animals includes fish, amphibians, reptiles, birds, and mammals. In fact, you are a vertebrate.

The largest animals on earth are vertebrates. Vertebrates can grow very large because they have an endoskeleton. This means the skeleton is on the inside of the body. The endoskeleton gives shape to and supports the animal's body. It also covers and protects the soft body parts. It grows as the body of the animal grows.

COMPREHENSION TEST SCIENCE

Name: ______________________ Date: ______________________

Animal Kingdom

Directions: Fill in the bubble next to the correct answer for each multiple-choice question.

1. What is the main idea of Passage One?
   - ◯ a. Some animals must shed their exoskeleton.
   - ◯ b. Some animals do not have backbones.
   - ◯ c. Some animals have highly developed brains.
   - ◯ d. Some animals have backbones.

2. What is the best antonym for the word **complex** as it is used in Passage Two?
   - ◯ a. difficult
   - ◯ b. hard
   - ◯ c. simple
   - ◯ d. plentiful

3. Which of these is **not** a vertebrate?
   - ◯ a. frog
   - ◯ b. fish
   - ◯ c. crab
   - ◯ d. snake

4. How is an exoskeleton different than an endoskeleton?
   - ◯ a. An exoskeleton is shed by the animal as it grows.
   - ◯ b. An exoskeleton protects the animal's body.
   - ◯ c. An exoskeleton supports the animal's body.
   - ◯ d. An exoskeleton allows the animal to move.

5. Using information from both passages, explain the difference between invertebrates and vertebrates.

____

____

____

____

____

____

Short Passage **History**

Child Labor in Early Textile Mills

Samuel Slater's mill in Pawtucket, Rhode Island

The first American textile mill was built in 1793. Samuel Slater, an immigrant from England, built the cotton-spinning mill in Rhode Island. It was modeled after the British factory system. Textile mills would change New England from farming to an industrial region.

Slater hired about 30 workers in his mill. Almost all of them were children. Some were as young as seven years old. They were paid about 25 cents a week. At his company store, the workers would buy items they needed in exchange for money or credits they had earned.

Work in the factory began before sunrise and would finish after sunset. The mills were dirty and noisy. In the winter, they were cold and drafty. In the summer, they were hot and humid. The lint in the air caused many of the workers to develop lung diseases.

Children worked in the early textile mills.

The machines were easy to operate but dangerous. The long hours and working conditions made the workers sleepy and tired, causing accidents. Workers could lose a finger or arm if they didn't move fast enough.

Slater had onsite housing built for the children. Near the mills, he built churches and schools the children attended. He made sure that the schools taught the children what he wanted them to learn. Sunday was their only day off.

COMPREHENSION TEST **HISTORY**

Name: ______________________ Date: ______________________

Child Labor in Early Textile Mills

Directions: Fill in the bubble next to the correct answer for each multiple-choice question.

1. The reading selection is **mostly** about
   - ○ a. the working conditions of children in a textile mill.
   - ○ b. Samuel Slater, an immigrant from England.
   - ○ c. how workers spent their money at the company store.
   - ○ d. the importance of textile mills in New England.

2. The **lint** in the air caused many of the workers to develop lung diseases. What is the best definition for the word **lint** as it is used in the sentence above?
   - ○ a. reddish dust
   - ○ b. thick smoke
   - ○ c. cloth fibers
   - ○ d. humidity

3. What was the weekly pay for a mill worker?
   - ○ a. 30 cents
   - ○ b. $179.30
   - ○ c. $17.93
   - ○ d. 25 cents

4. Why did Samuel Slater build schools near his mills?
   - ○ a. He wanted an educated work force.
   - ○ b. He wanted to control what the schools taught the children.
   - ○ c. He wanted children to learn job safety rules.
   - ○ d. He wanted all the children who worked at the mill to attend school.

5. Explain why it was dangerous for children to work in textile mills. Use at least two details from the selection to support your answer.

____

____

____

____

____

____

Reading Selection 1 **History**

Children on the Oregon Trail

The Oregon Trail was the route settlers took from Independence, Missouri, to Oregon City, Oregon. It was about 2,000 miles long. The trip took about five or six months. The first large wagon train set off for Oregon in 1843. It was led by Jesse Applegate. The wagon train included 120 wagons; 1,000 people; 5,000 cattle; plus chickens, pigs, and dogs.

Families heading west knew that the trip would be long and dangerous. When parents died along the trail, children were usually adopted by another family. Orphans might be left with families at forts, missions, or small settlements along the way.

Children did not attend school while on the trail. Many children kept a diary or wrote letters. Letters could be sent back East from military posts located on the trail. Children practiced their reading skills by reading the Bible with their parents.

The trail was bumpy and rough. Riding in a covered wagon wasn't very comfortable. The wagons were packed with supplies, so there wasn't much room. Most children walked. This helped to lighten the load. The only time children got to ride in a wagon was if they were very young, very sick, or the weather was bad. Many nights they would sleep under the wagon, unless it was too wet or cold.

Children had many chores while on the trail. Some of their chores were caring for livestock, fetching water, and milking cows. They also took care of younger children, helped with the cooking, and washing the clothes. As children walked, they searched for berries and other edible plants. An important job was picking up firewood, or "buffalo chips," for fuel. Buffalo chips were dried buffalo manure. It burned much more quickly than wood. It took two to three bushels of buffalo chips to cook a meal.

Children had little time to play and had few toys. However, at night they did participate in singing and dancing around the campfire. They visited friends and played games like London Bridge, Leap Frog, and Flying Dutchman. They could skip stones across a river, hold running and jumping contests, or play hide-and-seek. They also made up word and rhyming games.

Name: ______________________ Date: ______________________

Children on the Oregon Trail

Directions: Fill in the bubble next to the correct answer for each multiple-choice question.

1. This selection is **mostly** about
   - ○ a. the chores children had while traveling on the Oregon Trail.
   - ○ b. how children on the Oregon Trail received schooling.
   - ○ c. the games children played while traveling on the Oregon Trail.
   - ○ d. the life of children traveling on the Oregon Trail.

2. Which of the following words is **not** a compound word?
   - ○ a. campfire
   - ○ b. livestock
   - ○ c. wagon
   - ○ d. firewood

3. How long was the Oregon Trail?
   - ○ a. 1,000 miles
   - ○ b. 1,843 miles
   - ○ c. 2,000 miles
   - ○ d. 5,000 miles

4. Dried buffalo chips were used for
   - ○ a. food.
   - ○ b. fish bait.
   - ○ c. cattle feed.
   - ○ d. fuel.

5. Explain why most children did not ride in a covered wagon on the trail. Use at least two details from the selection to support your answer.

____

____

____

____

____

____

Reading Selection 2 **History**

Leif the Lucky

Do you think Christopher Columbus was the first European to visit the Americas? If you answered yes, you would be wrong. Evidence suggests that Norsemen, or Vikings, from Scandinavia sailed from Greenland to Newfoundland. Here they set up a colony about 500 years before Columbus was even born.

Stories of the life and adventures of Viking explorers were handed down orally for about 200 years before being written. The original documents have been lost. Only copies written in the 1300s and 1400s remain.

Leif Erikson

One of the most famous Viking explorers was Leif Erikson. He was born in Iceland sometime around A.D. 970. His father was Erik the Red. Erik the Red moved from Norway to Iceland when he was young. About A.D. 985, Erik the Red got into trouble and was banished from Iceland for three years. He and a small crew set off to explore the area west of Iceland. We do not know if Leif went with his father. When Erik returned, he reported finding a new land with green fields. He named it Greenland. Erik convinced others to move with him and his family to the new land.

Erik the Red became one of Greenland's leaders. He sent Leif on a ship to Norway in A.D. 997 to take presents to King Olaf. Leif was to trade furs, walrus and narwhal ivory, woolens, live polar bears, and gyrfalcons for items the colonists needed. Some of the items they needed were iron, timber, and grains.

The colony in Greenland grew larger. The lack of trees for building ships and homes became a problem. The few trees that grew there were small and scrubby. Leif had heard stories of other lands beyond Greenland, lands with many large trees. Around the year A.D. 1000, Leif sailed in search of those lands.

The first place Leif and his crew landed was probably Baffin Island. Leif named it Helluland. Sailing southwest, they sighted Markland, which was probably the coast of Labrador. Finally, they came to a channel that led to a river. Leif named it Vinland which means "Land of Meadows." They spent the winter there. No one knows exactly where Leif and his crew landed. It could have been in northern Newfoundland or as far south as Cape Cod, Massachusetts.

On the voyage home the following spring, Leif and his crew rescued sailors. The sailors had been shipwrecked on an island off the coast of Greenland. Because of this event and his discovery of Vinland, he was nicknamed Leif the Lucky.

Leif never returned to the land he had discovered. When his father died, Leif became leader of the Greenland settlement. Each year on October 9th, we celebrate "Leif Erikson Day" to honor his life and explorations.

COMPREHENSION TEST **HISTORY**

Name: ______________________________ Date: ______________________

Leif the Lucky

Directions: Fill in the bubble next to the correct answer for each multiple-choice question.

1. Which of these is a fact from the selection?
   - ○ a. Leif sent Erik the Red to take presents to King Olaf in Norway.
   - ○ b. Erik the Red was the father of Leif Erikson.
   - ○ c Settlers of Greenland needed to trade for iron, ivory, and woolens.
   - ○ d. Erik the Red was banished from Norway.

2. Which word is a synonym for the word **convinced** as it is used in paragraph three of the selection?
   - ○ a. asked
   - ○ b. forced
   - ○ c. informed
   - ○ d. persuaded

3. Who was a famous Viking explorer?
   - ○ a. Christopher Columbus
   - ○ b. King Olaf
   - ○ c. Leif Erikson
   - ○ d. Vinland

4. According to paragraph five, why did Leif search for lands beyond Greenland?
   - ○ a. He wanted to sail to Cape Cod, Massachusetts, for the winter.
   - ○ b. He needed trees for building ships and homes.
   - ○ c. He thought Greenland had gotten too populated.
   - ○ d. He wanted to take presents to King Olaf.

5. Explain why Leif Erikson was nicknamed Leif the Lucky. Use details from the selection to support your answer.

____

____

____

____

____

Reading Selection 3 **History**

Education of Children in Ancient Athens

Athena was the Greek goddess of wisdom.

In ancient Athens, the father was the head of the household. One of his duties was to oversee the education of his children, especially his sons. The role of the mother was to take care of the home and to raise her children. Before the age of six, parents taught their children at home.

If you were a girl living in ancient Athens, you would not receive a formal education. Your mother would be your only teacher. From your mother, you would learn how to spin thread and weave it into cloth. She would teach you how to cook and clean and any other tasks necessary for taking care of a home and family. This would prepare girls to one day become wives and mothers. Only if the mother was literate or the family was wealthy would a girl learn how to read and write.

The education of boys in ancient Athens was very different. The government mandated it was the parents' responsibility to make sure their sons received an education. The cultural belief was that boys needed to be educated in order to be knowledgeable leaders, responsible citizens, and skilled soldiers.

All boys received some type of formal education from the ages of seven to fourteen. Schools outside the home were made up of a small group of boys. The instructors were educated Greek slaves or paid teachers. Wealthy families hired personal tutors for their children.

Classes were held in the mornings. In the beginning, boys were taught how to read, write, and do math. Later, they learned about music and poetry. It was important for Greeks to understand Greek literature. They believed this was a way to tell if someone was educated. The poems of the poet Homer were especially important. From his poems, boys learned about Greek heroes and gods. Greeks thought this built moral character. It was also important to learn how to speak in public. This was a necessary skill for men who wanted to hold public office.

A healthy mind and body were very important to the Greeks. It would also prepare boys to be good soldiers. In the afternoon, they attended a gymnasium where they practiced running, wrestling, throwing the discus, and sports games.

Schooling for boys from wealthy families would continue past the age of fourteen. Some parents paid high fees to traveling teachers known as sophists. Other boys studied under the leadership of teachers known as philosophers, who did not charge fees.

COMPREHENSION TEST **HISTORY**

Name: ______________________________ Date: ____________________

Education of Children in Ancient Athens

Directions: Fill in the bubble next to the correct answer for each multiple-choice question.

1. The purpose of paragraph two is to show girls
   - ○ a. were better educated than boys.
   - ○ b. were taught how to take care of a home and family.
   - ○ c. wanted to grow up to be wives and mothers.
   - ○ d. had to do more work than boys.

2. What does the word **literate** mean as it is used in paragraph two of the selection?
   - ○ a. educated
   - ○ b. wealthy
   - ○ c. prepared
   - ○ d. responsible

3. How is a sophist different from a philosopher?
   - ○ a. A sophist was paid for teaching.
   - ○ b. A sophist did not charge fees for teaching.
   - ○ c. A sophist was hired to teach girls.
   - ○ d. A sophist was a teacher.

4. Which activity took place in a gymnasium?
   - ○ a. learning poetry
   - ○ b. throwing the discus
   - ○ c. weaving cloth
   - ○ d. practicing public speaking

5. Explain why the government of ancient Athens believed it was important for boys to be educated. Use details from the selection to support your answer.

____

____

____

____

____

____

Reading Selection 4 **History**

Victory Gardens

During World War II, the slogan "V is for Victory" became very popular in the United States. The idea was started by Victor de Laveleye, a Belgian. He had escaped to England from occupied Belgium. During his radio broadcasts, he encouraged Belgians to write the "V" sign everywhere. This was a show of defiance against Nazi Germany. He ended each radio broadcast with the Morse code for "V."

The U. S. government bought much of the food grown on farms to feed the troops overseas. Some food items like sugar, butter, eggs, coffee, meat and canned goods had to be rationed by the government. To help the war effort, Americans were encouraged to plant gardens to have fresh produce. Some people dug up their backyards and planted a garden. Others planted gardens alongside railroad tracks and driveways, in parks, on rooftops, and in window boxes. Children planted large gardens in their schoolyards to supply their cafeterias. These gardens were called victory gardens.

The goal for planting a victory garden was to grow enough fresh produce for the use of your family and neighbors during the summer. If you had extra produce, it would be preserved by canning. You would then have vegetables during the winter months. You would not need to buy commercial canned goods. The commercial canned goods could then be saved for the troops.

Some people did not know how to grow gardens. The government, groups like 4-H, and schools helped by providing land, instructions, and seeds. The need to grow gardens was promoted through posters, billboards, and articles in newspapers and magazines. People believed that by growing their own vegetables, they were helping to win the war.

Comprehension Test **History**

Name: ______________________ Date: ______________________

Victory Gardens

Directions: Fill in the bubble next to the correct answer for each multiple-choice question.

1. The topic of this selection is
   - ◯ a. urban farming during World War I.
   - ◯ b. the life of Victor de Laveleye, a Belgian refugee.
   - ◯ c. growing victory gardens during World War II.
   - ◯ d. preserving food and buying commercial canned goods.

2. Which word is the **best** synonym for the word <u>defiance</u> as it is used in the selection?
   - ◯ a. meekness
   - ◯ b. compliance
   - ◯ c. rebellion
   - ◯ d. victory

3. Victory gardens were a solution for
   - ◯ a. food shortage.
   - ◯ b. commercial canned goods.
   - ◯ c. preserving food.
   - ◯ d. winning the war.

4. What slogan was popular in the United States during World War II?
   - ◯ a. "Fight the Good Fight"
   - ◯ b. "V is for Victory"
   - ◯ c. "Let's Win!"
   - ◯ d. "Food for Troops"

5. Explain why Americans were encouraged to grow victory gardens. Use two details from the selection to support your answer.

____

____

____

____

____

____

Paired Passages **History**

The Leaders of the Lewis and Clark Expedition

Passage One: Meriwether Lewis

Meriwether Lewis was born on August 18, 1774, on a large farm in Virginia. When he was five years old, his father became sick and died. He inherited the farm. Due to his young age, his uncle ran it for him until he was older. In 1780, his mother married John Marks. Mr. Marks would later move the family to Georgia.

There were no schools in Georgia. Lewis had time to hunt, fish, and roam the woods. He became a very good woodsman. His mother knew about plants that grew in the area. She showed him how to make medicines from them. At the age of thirteen, Lewis was sent to Virginia for schooling. He learned Latin, math, natural science, and grammar. At the age of eighteen, he went to Georgia and moved his family back to Virginia.

In 1794, Lewis enlisted as a private in the Virginia militia. Two years later, he joined the U.S. Army. By 1800, he had reached the rank of captain. While in the army, he was able to travel and gain knowledge of the western frontier. In 1801, Thomas Jefferson asked the army to relieve Lewis of active duty so he could become his private secretary. He was to retain his rank of captain. Jefferson asked Lewis in 1803 to lead the expedition to explore the Louisiana Purchase. He was to find a water route to the Pacific Ocean.

Passage Two: William Clark

William Clark was born in Virginia on August 1, 1770. He grew up on a plantation. He was the youngest of six sons. His brother, George Rogers Clark, was a famous Revolutionary War hero.

When Clark was fourteen years old, his family moved to Kentucky, where there were no schools. He spent much of his time roaming the woods and learning things from his older brothers. He was very good at hunting, fishing, tracking, camping, and land navigation.

In 1789, Clark enlisted in the army. Later, he was promoted to the rank of captain. While serving in Ohio, Meriwether Lewis became a member of a unit led by Clark. They respected each other and became friends. Years later, this connection would lead Lewis to ask Clark to be co-leader of the Corps of Discovery expedition. His frontier experience, knowledge of Native Americans, and map-making skills would make Clark a valuable member of the team.

COMPREHENSION TEST **HISTORY**

Name: ______________________ Date: ______________

The Leaders of the Lewis and Clark Expedition

Directions: Fill in the bubble next to the correct answer for each multiple-choice question.

1. In Passage One, which sentence is an opinion?
   - ◯ a. When he was five years old, his father became sick and died.
   - ◯ b. He became a very good woodsman.
   - ◯ c. He studied Latin, math, natural science, and grammar.
   - ◯ d. There were no schools in Georgia.

2. What is the synonym for the word **rank** as it is used in Passage One?
   - ◯ a. position
   - ◯ b. membership
   - ◯ c. file
   - ◯ d. column

3. In Passage Two, why did Lewis and Clark become friends?
   - ◯ a. They served in the army.
   - ◯ b. They were good hunters.
   - ◯ c. They wanted to see the ocean.
   - ◯ d. They respected each other.

4. What rank did Lewis and Clark both achieve while serving in the army?
   - ◯ a. private
   - ◯ b. captain
   - ◯ c. major
   - ◯ d. general

5. Explain how the lives of Meriwether Lewis and William Clark were alike. Use details from both passages to support your answer.

____

____

____

____

____

____

SHORT PASSAGE GEOGRAPHY

Rain Forest

The rain forest is a biome. A biome is a large geographical area with a distinct climate, plants, and animals. The earth is divided into several biomes. The tropical rain forest is a biome located near the equator.

Rain forests have a wet, warm climate. This makes the forests very humid. The temperatures reach 90 degrees each day. Almost every afternoon brings a thunderstorm with heavy rainfall. Annual rainfall totals can be 80 to 100 inches or more.

Forests of trees with broad leaves grow to heights of 100 feet or more. The leaves of the very tall deciduous trees form a canopy over the forest floor. The canopy blocks out the sunlight. This makes the forest floor very dark. Without sunlight, few plants grow on the forest floor. Some plants grow high up in the canopy where they can receive sunlight. Orchids and ferns are examples of these types of plants.

Many animals are found in the rain forest. Cougars, snakes, birds, and monkeys are only a few. However, like the plants, the animals had to adapt to survive. They seldom come down to the forest floor. These animals hunt, eat, and sleep in the forest canopy. There the food is plentiful, and they are safe.

COMPREHENSION TEST **GEOGRAPHY**

Name: ______________________________ Date: ____________________

Rain Forest

Directions: Fill in the bubble next to the correct answer for each multiple-choice question.

1. Why did the author write the selection?
   - ○ a. to inform
   - ○ b. to persuade
   - ○ c. to entertain
   - ○ d. to convince

2. Some had to **adapt** to spending most of their lives in the trees.
   What definition of **adapt** is used in the sentence above?
   - ○ a. learn
   - ○ b. like
   - ○ c. want
   - ○ d. adjust

3. Orchids and ferns grow high up in the canopy where they can
   - ○ a. get fresh air.
   - ○ b. receive sunlight.
   - ○ c. capture rainwater.
   - ○ d. attract insects.

4. From the selection, readers can tell
   - ○ a. tropical rain forests can be found all over the world.
   - ○ b. food is plentiful.
   - ○ c. many of the plants and animals live in trees.
   - ○ d. orchids and ferns are the only plants that grow in trees.

5. Explain why deciduous trees are an important part of the rain forest biome. Use details from the selection to support your answer.

____

____

____

____

____

____

Reading Selection 1 **Geography**

Rivers

In the beginning, people hunted animals and gathered plants for food. They had to move often. They were nomads; they had no permanent place to live. They moved to a new location whenever the food ran out or herds moved on to new grazing lands.

Nomads often set up camp near a water source. Rivers were a good source of clean water for cooking and drinking. People caught and ate fish from the rivers. They hunted the animals that came to the rivers to drink. Also, they gathered the plants that grew close to the rivers.

The land along rivers was very fertile, and the soil was a good place for growing crops. People learned how to plant crops and grow enough food to feed their families. There was also enough food and water to raise animals. As the hunter-gatherer way of life shifted to farming, people began to settle along or near rivers.

As time went on, the number of people who settled along the rivers increased. More and more people joined the settlements. They wanted to be near a good source of food and water. With more food available, more people could be fed.

Rivers became even more important. People realized rivers could be used to transport people and goods. People began trading food, clothing, and other items up and down the river. Trade between settlements grew. Rivers became trade routes. This created jobs, drawing even more people to the area. These settlements became important trade centers and eventually grew into towns and then cities.

Today, rivers are still a very important part of our lives. Rivers provide water for farming, manufacturing, and everyday use. Big rivers provide transportation. When dams are built across rivers, they provide electricity for our homes and industries. Dams help control flooding and create a place for camping and boating.

One of the most important rivers in the United States is the Mississippi River. It is 2,348 miles long and runs from Minnesota to the Gulf of Mexico. It carries almost half the freight transported on the nation's rivers.

Name: ______________________________ Date: ______________________

Rivers

Directions: Fill in the bubble next to the correct answer for each multiple-choice question.

1. The author most likely wrote this passage in order to
   - ○ a. show the importance of rivers.
   - ○ b. describe the nomadic way of life.
   - ○ c. explain why dams are built.
   - ○ d. identify the most important river.

2. The land along rivers was very **fertile**.
   In the sentence above, the word **fertile** means
   - ○ a. valuable.
   - ○ b. poor.
   - ○ c. rich.
   - ○ d. meager.

3. Dams were built for all the following reasons **except**
   - ○ a. flood control.
   - ○ b. electricity.
   - ○ c. recreation.
   - ○ d. trade routes.

4. Why did nomads set up camps near rivers?
   - ○ a. to gather plants
   - ○ b. to water crops
   - ○ c. to raise animals
   - ○ d. to trade goods

5. Explain why people first settled along rivers. Use details from the selection to support your answer.

____

____

____

____

____

____

Plate Tectonics

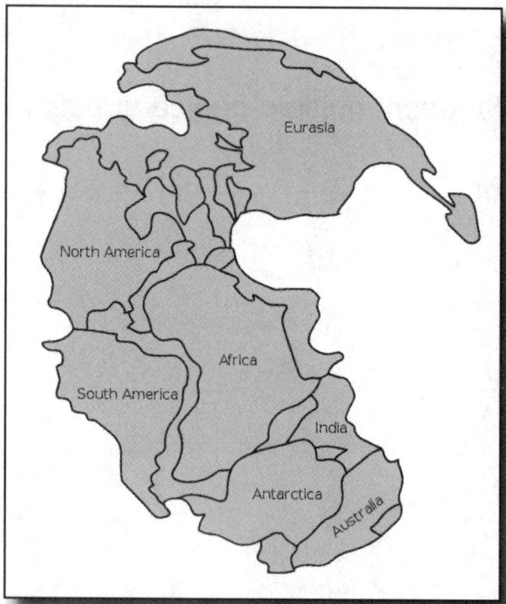

It is believed that Earth's seven continents once fit together like a jigsaw puzzle. Millions of years ago, the surface of the earth looked very different. The landform was one solid mass. This supercontinent is known as Pangaea. It broke apart and formed seven large plates called continents. These large, rigid slabs of solid rock slowly drifted to their present positions.

The Theory of Plate Tectonics

The movement of the plates can be explained by the Theory of Plate Tectonics. The plates are all moving in different directions and at different speeds. The motion of magma, just under the crust, causes the movement of the plates. They move from 2 cm to 10 cm per year. They can pull apart, move toward each other, or slide horizontally past each other. The place where the two plates meet is called a plate boundary. Interesting things can happen at the boundaries of these plates.

Plates Pull Apart

In the ocean where two plates pull apart, liquid rock can ooze up through the crack between the plates. This can form underwater volcanoes. The molten rock forms mountains as it cools and hardens. Sometimes these mountains are so high they stick out of the water. We call them islands. The Hawaiian Islands are a group of islands in the Pacific Ocean that were formed this way.

Plates Crash

In other places, where two plates are moving toward each other, one plate can dive under the other one. When this happens on the ocean floor, it forms a very deep ocean trench. In yet other places, land is forced upward when two plates move toward one another. An example of this would be in Asia where the crash of two plates has formed the Himalaya Mountains.

Plates Slide

The main boundary between the Pacific and North American plates is the San Andreas Fault in California. When the plates slide horizontally past each other, an earthquake can occur. One of the most famous earthquakes in this area was the San Francisco Earthquake of 1906.

COMPREHENSION TEST GEOGRAPHY

Name: ______________________ Date: ______________________

Plate Tectonics

Directions: Fill in the bubble next to the correct answer for each multiple-choice question.

1. The purpose of this selection is to
   - ◯ a. tell about underwater volcanoes.
   - ◯ b. describe mountain building.
   - ◯ c. explain the Theory of Plate Tectonics.
   - ◯ d. show how the seven continents were formed.

2. What is the meaning of the word horizontally as it is used in the selection?
   - ◯ a. to move up and down
   - ◯ b. to move in a circular motion
   - ◯ c. to move from corner to corner
   - ◯ d. to move straight across from side to side

3. When two plates move toward each other, it can create
   - ◯ a. mountains.
   - ◯ b. earthquakes.
   - ◯ c. islands.
   - ◯ d. continents.

4. Which subheading would you look under to find out what happens when an earthquake occurs?
   - ◯ a. The Theory of Plate Tectonics
   - ◯ b. Plates Pull Apart
   - ◯ c. Plates Crash
   - ◯ d. Plates Slide

5. Explain how the movement of the earth's plates formed the seven continents. Use two details from the selection to support your answer.

____

____

____

____

____

____

Reading Selection 3 **Geography**

Geography of the Thirteen Original Colonies

The thirteen British colonies are divided into three geographical regions. The regions are known as the New England, Middle, and Southern colonies. The natural features, climate, and natural resources of each region were major factors in the types of goods that were produced and traded.

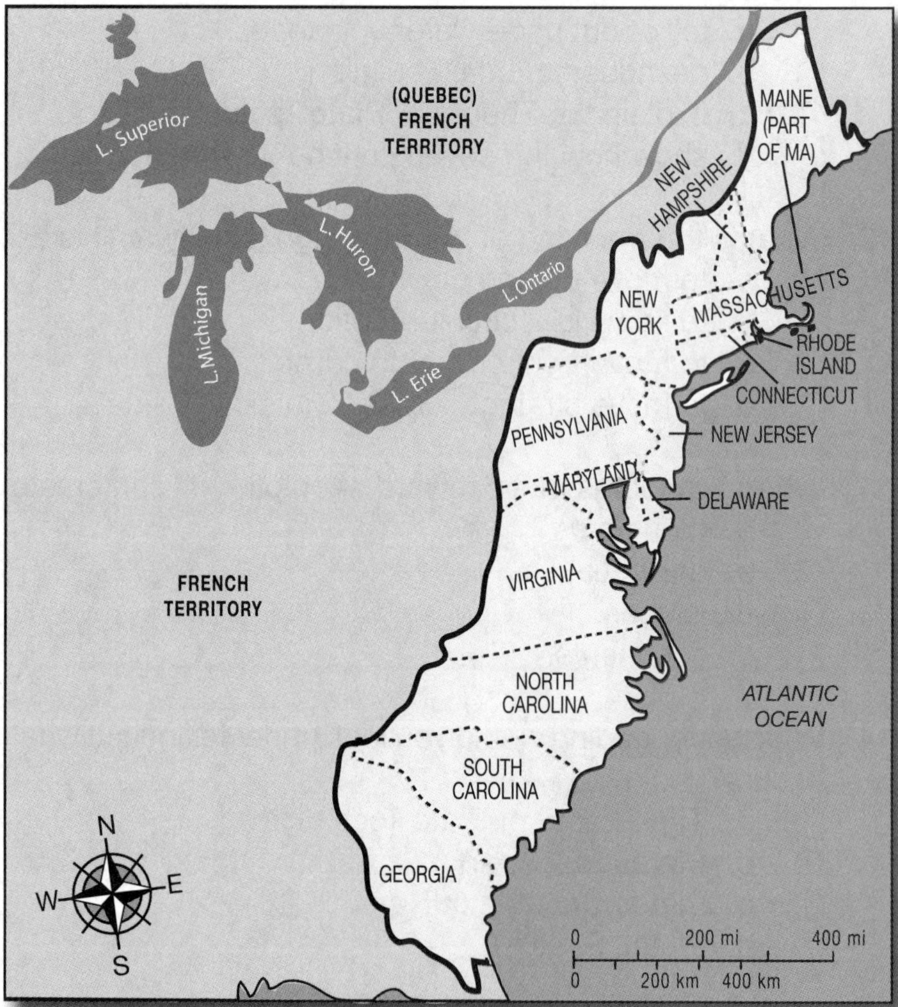

The land of the New England colonies was hilly with rocky soil. The cold climate caused a short growing season. This meant that the colonists had to depend upon the natural resources of fish, whales, trees, and furs. The trees provided lumber for shipbuilding. The depth of the continental shelf created a great fishing ground. Fishing, whaling, shipbuilding, and lumbering flourished.

The land of the Middle colonies was hilly, but there were also large areas of flat lands. The warm climate and rich soil was good for farming. Farmers were able to grow large amounts of wheat and other grains. This region became known as the "breadbasket colonies." Factories produced iron, paper, and textile products.

The land of the Southern colonies was a broad, coastal plain that was hilly and covered in forests. These colonies had the warmest climate of the three regions. The natural resources of these colonies included rich farm lands, forests, and fish. Since the soil was great for growing, colonists did not need to use other natural resources to develop industries. Instead they had large farms called plantations where tobacco, rice, and indigo were grown. The farms were worked by indentured servants and slaves.

COMPREHENSION TEST **GEOGRAPHY**

Name: ______________________ Date: ______________________

Geography of the Thirteen Original Colonies

Directions: Fill in the bubble next to the correct answer for each multiple-choice question.

1. In this nonfiction selection, the author mainly
   - ◯ a. tells about natural resources of the thirteen colonies.
   - ◯ b. shows the effects of warm climate and good soil.
   - ◯ c. describes the three geographic regions of the thirteen colonies.
   - ◯ d. encourages readers to find out more about life in the colonies.

2. What is the synonym for the word <u>region</u> as it is used in the selection?
   - ◯ a. area
   - ◯ b. large
   - ◯ c. resource
   - ◯ d. colony

3. Which of the following is **not** a natural resource?
   - ◯ a. money
   - ◯ b. fish
   - ◯ c. trees
   - ◯ d. soil

4. Why was farming **not** a major industry in the New England colonies?
   - ◯ a. depth of the continental shelf
   - ◯ b. cold climate and short growing season
   - ◯ c. warm climate and rich soil
   - ◯ d. covered with forests

5. Explain why the Middle colonies were also known as the "breadbasket colonies." Use details from the selection to support your answer.

____

____

____

____

____

____

Reading Selection 4 **Geography**

Geography of the United States

To understand the settlement and growth of the United States you need to know its geography. Geography is the study of the surface of the earth and the use of the land. Let's begin our study with the location and natural features of the United States.

North America, South America, and Antarctica are the three continents in the Western Hemisphere. The United States is one of three major countries on the continent of North America. To the north of the United States is Canada. To the south of the United States is Mexico.

In area, the United States is the fourth largest country in the world. It has an area of 3,615,122 square miles. It covers the full width of the North American continent. It extends from the Atlantic Ocean to the Pacific Ocean. It includes Alaska on the edge of the Arctic Circle and Hawaii far out in the Pacific Ocean.

The United States has fifty states. Forty-eight of the states cover area between Canada and Mexico. This group is known as the continental or lower 48 states. The states of Alaska and Hawaii are not part of the continental United States.

Oceans form a natural boundary for a large part of the United States. On the east is the Atlantic Ocean. On the west is the Pacific Ocean. Much of the southeastern United States borders on the Gulf of Mexico.

The United States has three major mountain ranges. The Appalachian Mountains are in the east. The Rocky Mountains lie in the interior of the United States. The Pacific Coast Range runs north and south through California, Oregon, and Washington.

Rivers and lakes are an important part of American life. They are used as a source of water and for the shipping of goods. When dams are built across rivers, they provide electricity for our homes and industries. The largest river in the United States is the Mississippi River. It runs the length of the United States from Canada to the Gulf of Mexico. In the north are the Great Lakes. These are five connecting lakes. They form the largest freshwater system on the earth's surface.

There are three major deserts in the United States. They are located in the western half of the country. These places receive less than ten inches of rainfall a year.

Knowing the geography of the United States is important. It will help when learning about our nation's growth and settlement patterns.

Name: ______________________ Date: ______________

Geography of the United States

Directions: Fill in the bubble next to the correct answer for each multiple-choice question.

1. This selection is **mostly** about
   - ○ a. the location and natural features of the United States.
   - ○ b. the rivers and lakes of the United States.
   - ○ c. the interior of the United States.
   - ○ d. the three major mountain ranges of the United States.

2. The word **interior** means
   - ○ a. to be placed.
   - ○ b. to be inside.
   - ○ c. to be outside.
   - ○ d. to be near.

3. What forms the natural boundary for a large part of the United States?
   - ○ a. rivers
   - ○ b. oceans
   - ○ c. mountains
   - ○ d. deserts

4. Which state is not part of the "lower 48 states"?
   - ○ a. Oregon
   - ○ b. Washington
   - ○ c. California
   - ○ d. Alaska

5. Explain why rivers and lakes are an important part of American life. Use details from the selection to support your answer.

____

____

____

____

____

____

PAIRED PASSAGES GEOGRAPHY

Ocean Currents and the Fishing Industry

Passage One: Grand Banks

Ocean currents are very important to the fishing industry in North America. All oceans have large currents. Currents are streams of water that move through the oceans like great rivers. In many places, the currents produce an upwelling of water from far below the ocean's surface. The upwelling water brings nutrients near the surface, which provides food for many fish. This creates rich fishing grounds.

The Grand Banks is a rich fishing area located in the North Atlantic just off the coast of Newfoundland. Fishing fleets from many parts of the world come to the Grand Banks to fish. The region around the Grand Banks is often shrouded in dense fog. This is very dangerous for fishing fleets in the area.

Passage Two: The Peru Current

In the Pacific Ocean along the west coast of South America, there are rich fishing grounds. Most years, there is a plentiful supply of fish. The fish feed on the rich nutrients brought to the ocean's surface by the upwelling of cold water. The cold water comes from the Peru Current, a river of cold water in the Pacific Ocean. The cold water comes to the surface because of trade winds that blow from the coast of South America toward the west and Asia. Fish then come to the area off the coast of Peru and Ecuador to feed.

In some years, however, the trade winds do not blow west from the coast near Peru and Ecuador. When this happens, there is no upwelling of cold water from below the ocean surface. When there is no upwelling of cold water, there is no food for the fish. The fish do not come to the coastal area to feed. This brings hardship to fishermen and their families, since there are no fish to be caught and sold.

Comprehension Test **Geography**

Name: ______________________________ Date: ____________________

Ocean Currents and the Fishing Industry

Directions: Fill in the bubble next to the correct answer for each multiple-choice question.

1. According to Passage One, ocean currents are like
   - ○ a. fishing grounds.
   - ○ b. upwelling water.
   - ○ c. great rivers.
   - ○ d. fishing fleets.

2. The region around the Grand Banks is often **shrouded** in dense fog. What does the word **shrouded** mean as it is used in the sentence above?
   - ○ a. covered
   - ○ b. revealed
   - ○ c. erased
   - ○ d. hampered

3. What is an **important** idea in both passages?
   - ○ a. Upwelling of water caused by ocean currents creates rich fishing grounds.
   - ○ b. When the trade winds do not blow, it causes hardships for the fishermen.
   - ○ c. Fishing is better in North America than South America.
   - ○ d. Fishing fleets come from many parts of the world to fish.

4. From these two passages, what conclusion can the reader make about ocean currents?
   - ○ a. Ocean currents affect the fishing industry.
   - ○ b. Fishing is a dangerous occupation.
   - ○ c. The fishing industry is important worldwide.
   - ○ d. Ocean currents all over the world produce rich fishing grounds.

5. Ocean currents are very important to the fishing industry. Do you agree or disagree? Use information from both passages to support your answer.

____

____

____

____

____

____

Short Passage Economics

Bartering

People have not always used money to buy what they wanted or needed. Thousands of years ago, people were nomads. They would move around, hunting and gathering food. Later, they settled in one area and began to farm. When they grew extra food, they would trade it for other items. To trade items without money is called bartering.

Early explorers traded blankets, beads, and tools to Native Americans for furs. More people began wanting items made of fur. Trading posts were set up to make it easier to trade the pelts. People made lots of money trapping and trading.

Bartering played a major role in the economy of colonial America. Colonies were not allowed to print paper money, so they bartered with items they had on hand. Sometimes the tobacco and corn they grew were used as trade items. This was a way for colonists to pay debts and buy goods.

As settlers pushed further and further west, bartering helped build friendships with the Native Americans. The journals of the Lewis and Clark Expedition record many accounts of bartering for supplies. Members of the expedition wrote how they used shiny coat buttons and beads to trade for food.

Many people still use bartering to gain the items they need and want. Some jobs lend themselves to bartering. For example, a barber might trade a haircut for carpentry work on his shop. Today, people use online bartering websites. This saves them money and time.

COMPREHENSION TEST **ECONOMICS**

Name: ______________________ Date: ______________

Bartering

Directions: Fill in the bubble next to the correct answer for each multiple-choice question.

1. The passage suggests bartering
   - ○ a. is an alternative to using money for items people need or want.
   - ○ b. is better than using money.
   - ○ c. is the reason the west was explored by Lewis and Clark.
   - ○ d. can be used to gain all the items people need or want.

2. Bartering played a major role in the **economy** of colonial America. What definition of the word **economy** is used in the sentence above?
   - ○ a. savings plan
   - ○ b. nation building
   - ○ c. trading goods
   - ○ d. financial system

3. According to the passage, which two items were used for bartering by the Lewis and Clark Expedition?
   - ○ a. tobacco and corn
   - ○ b. blankets and beads
   - ○ c. beads and buttons
   - ○ d. furs and pelts

4. What is another possible title for this selection?
   - ○ a. Needs and Wants
   - ○ b. Money in the Colonies
   - ○ c. Save Money and Time
   - ○ d. Trading Without Spending Money

5. Explain how bartering is used today. Use details from the passage to support your answer.

____

____

____

____

____

____

READING SELECTION 1 **ECONOMICS**

Goods and Services

Where do you live? Is it on a farm? Maybe it is in an apartment building in a large city? Wherever it is, the area that surrounds you is your community, or neighborhood. Within your community, many goods and services are available. Goods and services are the products that satisfy your needs and wants.

What are Goods?

Goods are items that we use. They are things that can be touched. Some examples of goods are clothing, bicycles, breakfast cereals, and computers. Some goods are bought to be used once. A candy bar would be an example of this type of good. Cars are goods that are purchased with the idea that they will be used over and over again. You can purchase goods, but some goods do not cost anything. If someone gives you a book, then you have received a good. It didn't cost you anything, because you didn't pay for the book.

Types of Goods

There are three important types of goods. Goods that people want or need are known as consumer goods. These are items such as food and cars. Businesses purchase raw materials and tools used to make consumer goods. The raw materials are known as producer goods. For example, a candy company might purchase nuts to put in a candy bar. The nuts would be producer goods. Another type of goods is capital goods. They are used to make producer goods. The machine that the candy company uses to mix the candy bar recipe would be a capital good.

Imports and Exports

Not all of our goods are made in our country. Goods that we buy from foreign countries are known as imports. Coffee beans and chocolate are examples of goods that are imported to the United States. Goods that we produce and send to other countries are known as exports. Corn and soybeans are agricultural goods that are exported by the United States.

What are Services?

Services are any actions that one person or group does for another. Services can include the use of goods. To send letters through the U.S. Postal Service, you must purchase goods. The goods are the stamps used to mail the letters. When a mail carrier delivers your letters, he or she is providing a service. Some types of services produce goods. A baker provides a service by baking a cake for your birthday party. The birthday cake is the goods produced. Sometimes you don't pay for services. In large cities, professional firefighters are hired to provide the service of fighting fires. However, in a rural area where there are not as many fires, community members volunteer their services to help fight fires.

Name: ______________________________ Date: ____________________

Goods and Services

Directions: Fill in the bubble next to the correct answer for each multiple-choice question.

1. Which sentence **best** states the main idea of this selection?
   - ○ a. There are three important types of goods.
   - ○ b. You can purchase goods and services.
   - ○ c. Within your community, goods and services are available.
   - ○ d. Goods and services are the products that satisfy your needs and wants.

2. The words **import** and **export** are
   - ○ a. synonyms.
   - ○ b. antonyms.
   - ○ c. homonyms.
   - ○ d. metaphors.

3. People who provide services without pay are
   - ○ a. consumers.
   - ○ b. producers.
   - ○ c. volunteers.
   - ○ d. members.

4. Which subheading would you look under to find out about capital goods?
   - ○ a. What are Goods?
   - ○ b. Types of Goods
   - ○ c. Imports and Exports
   - ○ d. What are Services?

5. Explain the difference between goods and services. Use details from the selection to support your answer.

____

____

____

____

____

____

Reading Selection 2 **Economics**

Banking

Banks provide people with a safe place to store their money. In earlier times, people left their coins with money exchangers and lenders who stored the coins in strongboxes. In Italy, banking was held on city street benches. The idea of banking spread to other countries.

In the 1600s, English goldsmiths acted as bankers. They stored coins for people in their vaults. Receipts were given for the deposits. These were easier to carry than coins. People began using the receipts as money.

In 1791, the United States Congress established the First Bank of the United States. Many states and individuals also owned and ran banks. Each bank printed its own bank notes or paper money. This is known as the "Free Banking Era." Many of the banks printed too much paper money. This created a financial panic. People began to distrust the banks.

In 1913, Congress established the Federal Reserve note. It became the only legal U.S. currency. In the 1930s, the stock market crashed and many banks failed. This era is known as the Great Depression. In March of 1933, President Franklin D. Roosevelt ordered a nationwide banking holiday. This meant that all the banks were to be closed. This stopped people from trying to change their bank deposits into gold or cash. The president believed that it would give the banks time to recover. Banks that were financially sound were allowed to reopen.

The Federal Deposit Insurance Corporation (FDIC) was created by the United States Congress. The purpose of the FDIC was to help restore faith in the banking industry by protecting a depositor's money.

Today, banks offer a wide range of services for customers. Money can be deposited at banks in a variety of accounts. Checking accounts allow depositors to withdraw their money. This can be done through ATM machines, debit cards, automatic payment withdrawals, and/or writing checks. People must have enough money in their accounts to cover the money withdrawn. If not, they must pay an overdraft fee.

Savings accounts allow people to store their money at the bank. In return, the bank pays the depositor interest for using their money. The bank uses the money to make loans and earns money by charging interest on the loans. A bank can also make money by charging fees for checking accounts, ATM withdrawals, and overdrafts.

Name: ______________________ Date: ______________________

Banking

Directions: Fill in the bubble next to the correct answer for each multiple-choice question.

1. This selection is **mostly** about
   - ○ a. the FDIC.
   - ○ b. the Great Depression.
   - ○ c. the history of banking.
   - ○ d. the Free Banking Era.

2. Banks that were financially **sound** were allowed to reopen.
   What definition of the word **sound** is used in the sentence above?
   - ○ a. secure
   - ○ b. announce
   - ○ c. noise
   - ○ d. legal

3. The purpose of having a savings account is to
   - ○ a. charge interest.
   - ○ b. make loans.
   - ○ c. earn money.
   - ○ d. store money.

4. Congress established the Federal Reserve Note in
   - ○ a. 1791. ○ b. 1913.
   - ○ c. 1930. ○ d. 1933.

5. Explain why President Franklin D. Roosevelt ordered a nationwide banking holiday. Use details from the selection to support your answer.

____

____

____

____

____

____

READING SELECTION 3 **ECONOMICS**

Income Tax

The first federal income tax was collected in 1862. Its purpose was to help pay the cost of the United States Civil War. Before the Civil War, the U.S. government did not tax income. Instead, it relied on revenues from **tariffs** on imported goods. When the war came to an end, the tax was repealed.

The government returned to using tariffs and taxing items such as beer, tobacco, and even chewing gum to raise revenue. Congress realized these types of taxes were not reliable sources of revenue. The Sixteenth Amendment was passed in 1913. It gave the government the power to impose and collect income tax.

An **income tax** is a tax on the money an individual or business earns each year. Cities, states, and/or the federal government collect the tax. The government has set up a method of tax withholding. It makes the payment and collection of personal income taxes easier for taxpayers. Employers withhold a certain amount of money from each employee's paycheck. A rate table is used to know the amount to be withheld. The money is sent to the appropriate government.

People are given a pay slip each time they are paid. The pay slip shows how much money has been earned and how much tax has been withheld from the paycheck. The pay slip is a record for the employee. It shows earnings and deductions.

Each year the deadline for paying personal income tax is April 15. Taxpayers are required to submit a tax return to the Internal Revenue Service (IRS). Some taxpayers may still owe income tax at the end of the year. Other taxpayers may receive a tax **refund**. This depends on whether the employer has withheld too little or too much money from an employee's paycheck.

Many people send their tax returns through the post office. Some taxpayers use electronic filing. It is faster and more convenient. The IRS receives the tax return and checks to make sure it is correct. If you overpaid, they will send you a refund. It is illegal to avoid paying your taxes.

Comprehension Test **Economics**

Name: ____________________ Date: ____________________

Income Tax

Directions: Fill in the bubble next to the correct answer for each multiple-choice question.

1. Which text feature is used to focus the reader's attention on important words in the selection?
   - ○ a. italics
   - ○ b. boldface
   - ○ c. underlining
   - ○ d. color

2. What is the synonym for the word **tariffs** as used in the selection?
   - ○ a. refunds
   - ○ b. fines
   - ○ c. taxes
   - ○ d. donations

3. Taxpayers are required to submit a tax return
   - ○ a. to the IRS.
   - ○ b. to Congress.
   - ○ c. to employers.
   - ○ d. to cities.

4. Some taxpayers receive an income tax refund because
   - ○ a. too much money was withheld from their paychecks.
   - ○ b. too little money was withheld from their paychecks.
   - ○ c. it is faster and more convenient.
   - ○ d. it shows earnings and deductions.

5. Explain the purpose of a pay slip. Use details from the selection to support your answer.

____

____

____

____

____

____

Reading Selection 4 **Economics**

Trade-offs and Opportunity Cost

Do you have enough money to buy everything you want? If not, you will have to decide which items to buy. The economic term for making these decisions is called trade-offs. Trade-offs means that you give up something of value to get what is most wanted. Sometimes your choice can be the resource of time. For example, you may have to choose whether you want to spend time playing a game with your friend or spend the time studying for a test. At other times, your choice may involve money. Do you buy a candy bar or save for a cell phone?

When you make an economic decision, you run the risk of not making the best choice. The opportunity cost of a decision is what is given up when the other choice is not selected. The opportunity cost of deciding to spend one hour studying for a math test, might be the lost opportunity to spend time with friends. The risk is whether the extra time studying will result in a higher test score.

There are steps to follow when making economic decisions. Let's consider that your economic decision is: How to spend a Saturday afternoon. First, make a list of the criteria needed to make the decision. Do you need to earn money? Maybe you want to spend the afternoon playing outdoors.

Next, list all possible choices. One choice might be to go skateboarding with friends. Another might be to spend the afternoon earning money mowing lawns. After listing all your choices, consider the pros and cons of each. Then rank your choices in the order of which one you want or need to do most.

Finally, make your choice and identify the opportunity cost of this decision. Was your top choice to earn money by mowing the lawn? If so, the opportunity cost of this decision is what you ranked second.

Governments provide citizens with some goods and services they are not able to provide for themselves. The opportunity cost of decisions may result in little or no funding to other budget items. For example, fully funding national defense might result in less money for fixing highways.

Business leaders always have to consider trade-offs and opportunity cost when making economic decisions. For example, when a business earns a profit, what are they going to do with it? Should they save the money, give their workers a raise, or buy new equipment? Making good economic decisions helps a business to be successful.

COMPREHENSION TEST **ECONOMICS**

Name: ______________________________ Date: ______________________

Trade-offs and Opportunity Cost

Directions: Fill in the bubble next to the correct answer for each multiple-choice question.

1. This passage is **mostly** about
   - ○ a. making economic decisions.
   - ○ b. how to spend your money.
   - ○ c. how to spend a Saturday afternoon.
   - ○ d. making a profit.

2. The best definition for the word **profit** as it is used in the last paragraph of the selection is
   - ○ a. money left over after all expenses are paid.
   - ○ b. a religious person who foretells the future.
   - ○ c. what business leaders always have to consider when making decisions.
   - ○ d. what helps you decide which item to purchase.

3. According to the selection, who provides citizens with some goods and services they are not able to provide for themselves?
   - ○ a. business leaders ○ b. government
   - ○ c. consumers ○ d. producers

4. The opportunity cost of a decision is
   - ○ a. what is given up when the other choice is not selected.
   - ○ b. to earn a profit from selling an item.
   - ○ c. deciding how to spend your time.
   - ○ d. what is gained from spending time with a friend.

5. Describe the steps to follow when making an economic decision. Use details from the selection to support your answer.

____

____

____

____

____

____

Needs and Wants

Passage One: Needs

The basic needs for human survival are air, water, food, clothing, and shelter. Needs are something you must have in order to survive. We may be able to go for a brief time without water, but eventually without it we would die. If you prefer to drink flavored water, then the flavored water becomes a want, not a need.

Sometimes we confuse needs with necessities. Let's consider whether or not electricity is a need. How do we use electricity? Maybe it provides power to a pump that fills a community's water tank. It could power a stove used to prepare food for meals. So is electricity a need? Could we survive without it? Of course we could. We would prefer not to because it would change our lifestyle and make our life less easy. So electricity is not a need, but in our society it is considered a necessity.

Consumers are people who purchase things they need and want. They have economic needs that are determined by their situation or circumstance. As a student, you have probably heard a teacher say that you must come to class prepared. This usually means that you are to bring certain items to class each day, such as a pencil. In this situation, a pencil is a necessity.

Passage Two: Wants

Most people would agree that humans have lots of wants. Wants are luxuries that we would like to have but could live without. They are not necessary for our survival. Food is something we need to survive. It contains vitamins and minerals that are essential for good health. When we prefer a certain type of food, it becomes a want. Some people enjoy eating steak. While steak may taste good and contain vitamins, we don't need steak to survive.

Have you ever heard the term *"economic wants"*? We can fulfill our economic wants with goods and services. Goods are items that we use. They are things that can be touched. Services are any actions that one person or group does for another. Most of us have access to a variety of goods and services. Sometimes the items we want may cost more than we can afford to spend. We may have to save our money to purchase these luxuries.

Smart consumers learn to make good choices. They know the difference between necessities and luxuries. They understand that advertisements are used to make goods and services more appealing to consumers. Advertisers try to convince people that they need an item, when really that item is a want or luxury.

Name: ______________________________ Date: ____________________

Needs and Wants

Directions: Fill in the bubble next to the correct answer for each multiple-choice question.

1. What is the main idea of Passage One?
   - ○ a. Goods are items that we use.
   - ○ b. Needs are something you must have in order to survive.
   - ○ c. Smart consumers learn to make good choices.
   - ○ d. Consumers are people who purchase things they need and want.

2. It could **power** a stove used to prepare food for meals.
   What is the meaning of the word **power** as it is used in the sentence above?
   - ○ a. physical strength
   - ○ b. muscle
   - ○ c. influence
   - ○ d. provide energy

3. In Passage Two, what can fulfill our economic wants?
   - ○ a. consumers and producers
   - ○ b. needs and necessities
   - ○ c. goods and services
   - ○ d. necessities and luxuries

4. Which item is a want?
   - ○ a. air ○ b. steak
   - ○ c. shelter ○ d. water

5. Explain the difference between needs and wants. Use details from the selection to support your answer.

   ____

   ____

   ____

   ____

   ____

   ____

SHORT PASSAGE **INFORMATIONAL TEXT**

George Washington Carver

George Washington Carver was born near Carthage, Missouri, sometime around 1864. His mother was a slave. At the age of nine, he set out on his own. Through the years, his schooling and self-education would make him the leading expert on crops in the South.

Carver is most famous for products he made from peanuts. He found over 300 uses for the peanut. He also found ways to utilize other crops, such as potatoes and pecans.

Carver's honors were many. He won honorary doctorates from Simpson College and the University of Rochester. In 1939, he received the Roosevelt Medal for Contributions to Southern Agriculture. These are only a few of the honors won by Carver in his late years. This was a notable life for a poor child born into slavery.

Timeline

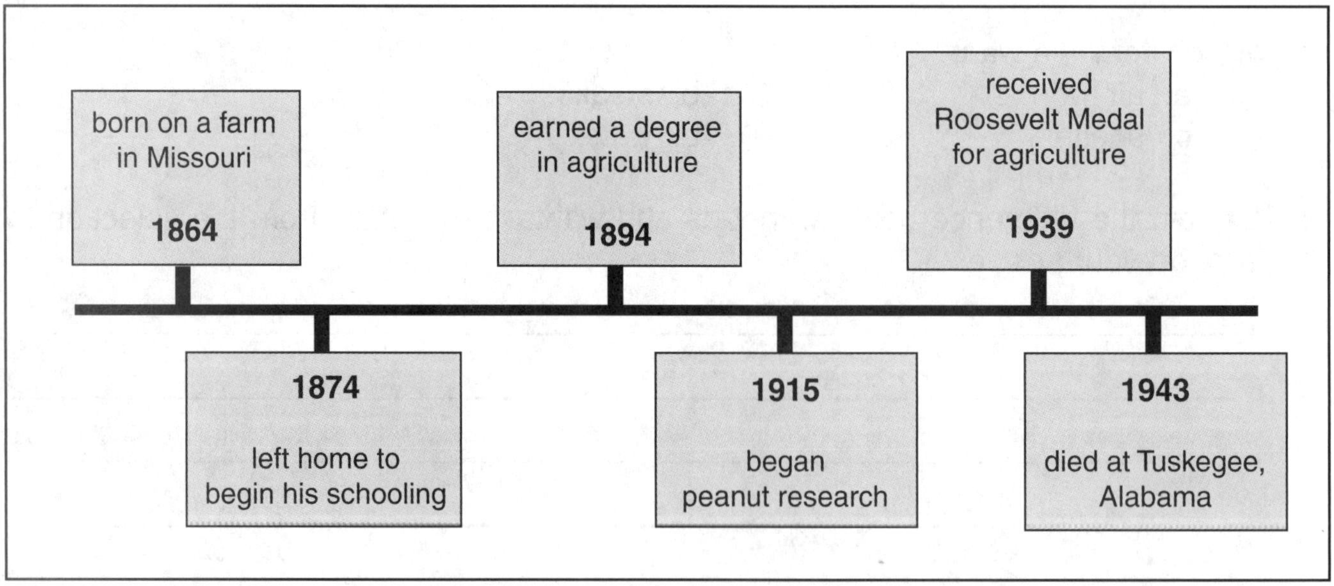

COMPREHENSION TEST **INFORMATIONAL TEXT**

Name: ______________________ Date: ______________

George Washington Carver

Directions: Fill in the bubble next to the correct answer for each multiple-choice question.

1. The timeline helps the reader to
   - ○ a. find out about products made from peanuts.
   - ○ b. learn how George Washington Carver became an expert on southern crops.
   - ○ c. get an overall picture of George Washington Carver's life.
   - ○ d. know who invented peanut butter.

2. According to the timeline, in which year did George Washington Carver leave home to begin his schooling?
   - ○ a. 1864
   - ○ b. 1874
   - ○ c. 1894
   - ○ d. 1915

3. According to the timeline, why did George Washington Carver receive the Roosevelt Medal?
   - ○ a. for peanut research
   - ○ b. for teaching
   - ○ c. for agriculture
   - ○ d. for potato research

4. Which important event does **not** appear on the timeline?
   - ○ a. He was born on a farm.
   - ○ b. He won an honorary doctorate from Simpson College.
   - ○ c. He died in Tuskegee, Alabama.
   - ○ d. He earned a degree in agriculture.

5. Why do you think the author used a timeline in this selection? Give details to support your answer.

____

____

____

____

____

____

READING SELECTION 1 **INFORMATIONAL TEXT**

Time Zones

When it became necessary to standardize time, scientists divided the earth into different time zones. Since there are 24 hours in a day, there are 24 different time zones. Scientists came up with this idea because the sun moves over each part of the earth at a different time of the day.

The contiguous United States is divided into four time zones: Eastern, Central, Mountain, and Pacific. The states of Alaska and Hawaii have their own time zones. Each of these time zones is one hour apart. When you are traveling in a westward direction, move your watch backward one hour. When you are traveling in an eastward direction, move your watch forward one hour.

United States Time Zone Map

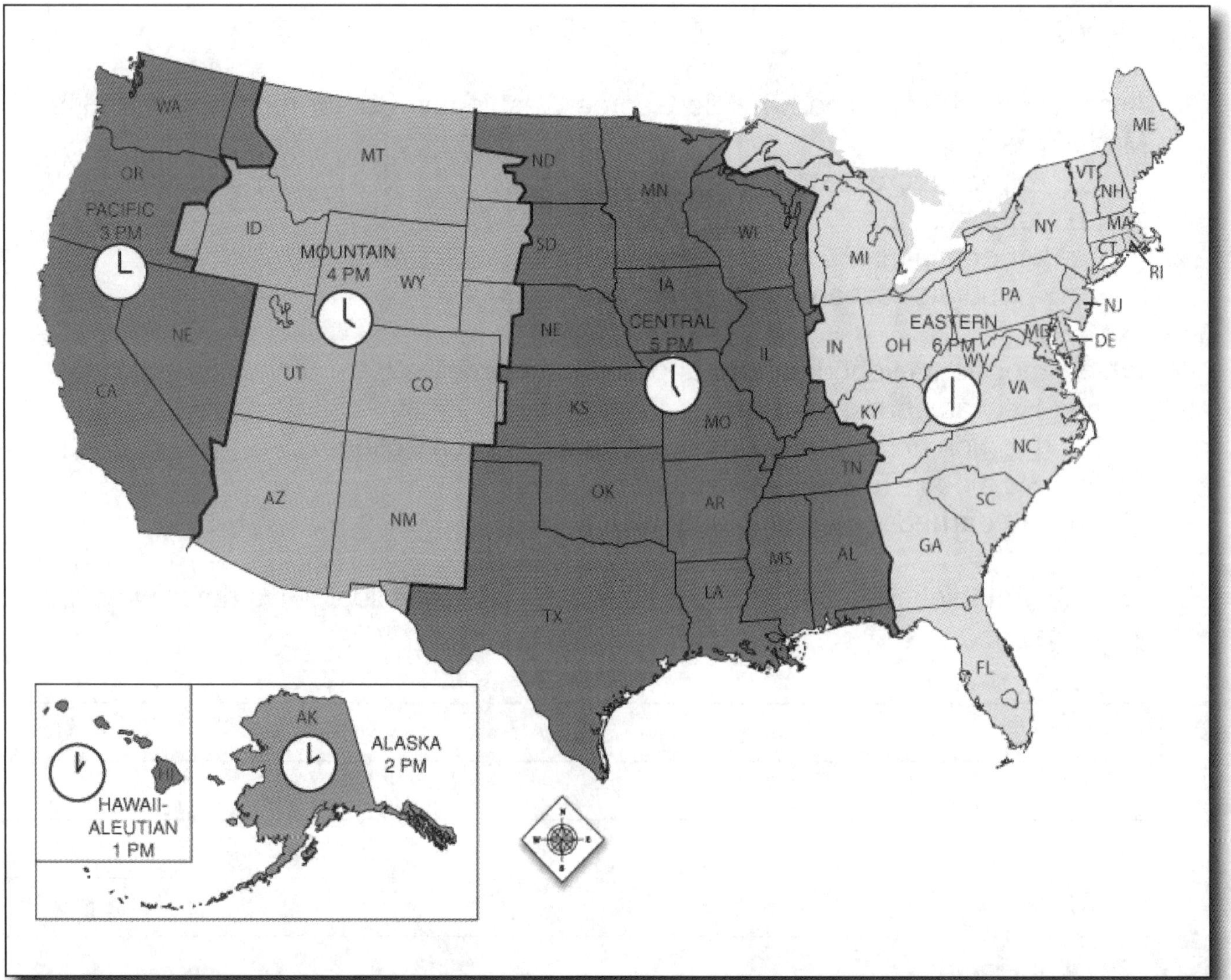

COMPREHENSION TEST **INFORMATIONAL TEXT**

Name: ______________________________ Date: ______________________

Time Zones

Directions: Fill in the bubble next to the correct answer for each multiple-choice question.

1. Which state is located in two time zones?
   - ◯ a. Georgia
   - ◯ b. Minnesota
   - ◯ c. Pennsylvania
   - ◯ d. Tennessee

2. Scientists divided the earth into
   - ◯ a. 6 time zones.
   - ◯ b. 12 time zones.
   - ◯ c. 24 time zones.
   - ◯ d. 48 time zones.

3. Ohio is located in which time zone?
   - ◯ a. Eastern
   - ◯ b. Central
   - ◯ c. Mountain
   - ◯ d. Pacific

4. If it is 3:00 P.M. in Iowa, what time is it in California?
   - ◯ a. 1:00 P.M.
   - ◯ b. 2:00 P.M.
   - ◯ c. 3:00 P.M.
   - ◯ d. 4:00 P.M.

5. How does the map help the reader to understand time zones? Give details to support your answer.

____

____

____

____

____

____

Reading Selection 2 **Informational Text**

Making Bones Bend

Our body needs calcium to build strong, healthy teeth and bones. During childhood and adolescence, bones grow the most. It is important to get enough calcium during these years. The more bone mass accumulated early in life, the less likely you are to develop a serious bone problem later in life.

Low calcium levels can cause the likelihood of broken bones, unhealthy teeth, and even rickets. As an adult, low levels of calcium can cause osteoporosis, a painful condition caused by the decrease in bone density or the amount of calcium in bones. The elderly may experience broken hips and other fractures with decreased bone density.

Building and maintaining strong bones depends on the mineral calcium. Without it, your bones would be bendable and would not be able to support your body. While many foods contain calcium, dairy products are the most significant source. Let's find out what happens when calcium is removed from bones.

Scientific Experiment

Supplies:

- uncooked chicken bone
- glass container, with lid
- distilled white vinegar

Directions:

Step 1. Clean the meat from an uncooked chicken bone and allow it to dry overnight.

Step 2. Place the bone in the glass container. Fill the container with vinegar until the bone is covered. Place a lid on the container.

Step 3. Allow the bone to sit in the vinegar for seven days. On the third day, drain the container, add fresh vinegar, and place the lid back on the container.

Step 4. After a week has passed, remove the bone from the vinegar. The bone should be flexible and easy to bend.

Caution: Chickens are carriers of bacteria such as salmonella. Wash your hands thoroughly with soap and water after handling raw chicken.

Comprehension Test **Informational Text**

Name: ______________________ Date: ______________

Making Bones Bend

Directions: Fill in the bubble next to the correct answer for each multiple-choice question.

1. What is the organizational structure of the directions for the experiment?
   - ○ a. chronological
   - ○ b. sequential
   - ○ c. cause-effect
   - ○ d. problem-solution

2. What does a person need to do **after** placing the bone in the glass container?
   - ○ a. remove the meat from the uncooked chicken bone
   - ○ b. wash hands with soap and water
   - ○ c. fill the container with vinegar
   - ○ d. place a lid on the container

3. In which section would a reader learn what to gather before experimenting with the chicken bones?
   - ○ a. Supplies
   - ○ b. Directions
   - ○ c. Steps
   - ○ d. Caution

4. According to the directions, how long are you to leave the bone in the vinegar?
   - ○ a. 1 day ○ b. 1 week
   - ○ c. 1 month ○ d. 1 year

5. According to the selection, what causes the chicken bone to become flexible and easy to bend? Use details from the selection to support your answer.

____

____

____

____

____

____

Reading Selection 3 **Informational Text**

Conestoga Wagons

In the 1860s, many families decided to join a wagon train and move to Oregon. The wagon train was led by an experienced guide who knew the best route west. The wagon train traveled 15 to 20 miles a day. The trip took approximately six months.

Many families chose to travel in a large, sturdy wagon with high sides called a Conestoga. This type of wagon was considered the best and was the most expensive. They used horses, mules, or oxen to pull the wagons. The wagons were designed for hauling freight on the east coast. They were sturdy, well-built wagons. This made them suitable for traveling along the Santa Fe or Oregon Trail.

Conestoga wagons were nicknamed "prairie schooners." The high, white canvas tops looked like sailing ships as they crossed the sea of grass on the American prairie. The strong, broad wheels allowed the wagons to cross rutted roads, muddy flats, and the non-roads of the prairie. The curved floor was designed to reduce load shifting. Conestogas were capable of hauling loads up to six tons.

Diagram

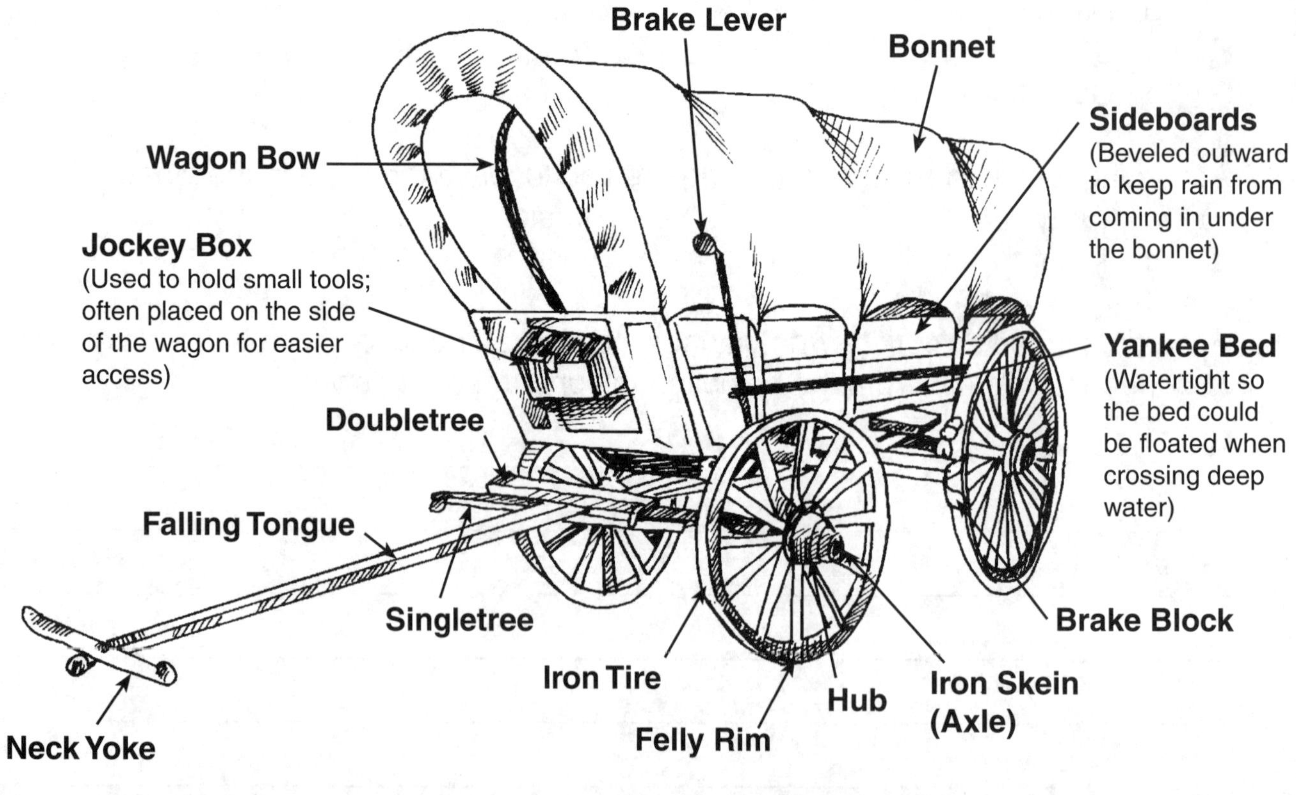

COMPREHENSION TEST INFORMATIONAL TEXT

Name: ______________________ Date: ______________________

Conestoga Wagons

Directions: Fill in the bubble next to the correct answer for each multiple-choice question.

1. The purpose of the diagram is to help the reader
   - ○ a. learn why Conestoga wagons were nicknamed "prairie schooners."
   - ○ b. learn about the parts of a Conestoga wagon.
   - ○ c. understand why Conestoga wagons were designed to haul freight.
   - ○ d. understand why the Conestoga was the best and most expensive wagon.

2. According to the diagram, which of the following is **not** a part of a wagon wheel?
   - ○ a. felly rim
   - ○ b. hub
   - ○ c. axle
   - ○ d. singletree

3. What was the purpose for beveling the sideboards on a Conestoga wagon?
   - ○ a. to help the bed float when crossing deep water
   - ○ b. for easy access to small tools
   - ○ c. to keep rain from coming in under the bonnet
   - ○ d. for holding the water barrels in place

4. In the diagram, the canvas top of the Conestoga wagon is labeled
   - ○ a. bonnet
   - ○ b. brake lever
   - ○ c. wagon bow
   - ○ d. sideboards

5. Explain why the Conestoga was considered to be the best wagon for traveling the Oregon Trail. Use two details from the selection to support your answer.

____

____

____

____

____

____

Paired Passages **Informational Text**

School Uniforms

Passage One: Student Editorial 1

Our school is thinking about requiring students to wear uniforms. I think this is a good idea. There are many good reasons why students should be required to wear school uniforms, but I want to focus on two main reasons.

School uniforms would help reduce peer pressure. Students feel to be accepted they have to wear the latest fashion trends. If not, they are afraid they are going to be bullied or made to feel like an outcast. This can cause some students to get upset, frustrated, or have low self-esteem. If everyone is wearing the same type of clothes, no one can be judged by what they wear. My character and how I treat others becomes more important than how I look.

School uniforms would prepare students for working in the real world. Some businesses have dress codes for their workers. Many jobs require you to wear uniforms. My dad is a police officer, and he has to wear a uniform to work every day. Our job is to be students. A uniform will remind us about our purpose for being at school.

I support the idea of wearing school uniforms. In my opinion, it will improve the attitudes of students and prepare them for a career.

Passage Two: Student Editorial 2

During our class meeting, the principal talked to us about a possible new school rule. We were told all middle-school students would have to wear school uniforms. I do not think this is a good idea.

I like to express my individual style and personality through the clothes I choose to wear. I don't want to be forced to look like everyone else. If I am required to wear a school uniform, then I lose my freedom to choose.

Some people think school uniforms will save parents money. I don't believe this is true. I think it will cause parents to spend more money. Parents will still have to buy clothing for the hours we are not in school. Instead of saving money, parents will be spending more.

These are just a few of the reasons I hope we do not have to wear school uniforms. I hope our principal considers my viewpoint before making the final decision.

Comprehension Test **Informational Text**

Name: ______________________________ Date: ______________________

School Uniforms

Directions: Fill in the bubble next to the correct answer for each multiple-choice question.

1. What is the main idea of Student Editorial 1?
   - ◯ a. School uniforms are a good idea for middle-school students.
   - ◯ b. School uniforms reduce bullying and peer pressure.
   - ◯ c. School uniforms make students feel like outcasts.
   - ◯ d. School uniforms cause low self-esteem.

2. **If I am required to wear a school uniform, then I lose my freedom to choose.** Which persuasive device is the student using in the sentence above?
   - ◯ a. bandwagon ◯ b. loaded words
   - ◯ c. repetition ◯ d. testimonial

3. Why did the students write the editorials?
   - ◯ a. to inform
   - ◯ b. to entertain
   - ◯ c. to describe
   - ◯ d. to persuade

4. What conclusion can the reader make about the two students who wrote the editorials?
   - ◯ a. Both students have strong feelings about wearing school uniforms.
   - ◯ b. Both students like the idea of wearing school uniforms.
   - ◯ c. Both students dislike the idea of wearing school uniforms.
   - ◯ d. Both students feel wearing uniforms will save parents money.

5. In your opinion, which student editorial is **more** convincing? Use details from the selection to support your answer.

____

____

____

____

____

____

Answer Keys

Earthquakes (p. 3)
1. d, 2. c, 3. a, 4. c, 5. If structures aren't built properly, earthqakes can bring down buildings and bridges; destroy highways; break gas lines; and cause loss of human life

Amphibians (p. 5)
1. b, 2. c, 3. a, 4. d, 5. Can't produce their own body heat; when the temperature around them is cold, they become cold and lazy as body functions slow down.

Magnets (p. 7)
1. c, 2. b, 3. a, 4. a, 5. A permanent magnet holds its magnetic properties over time; a temporary magnet will lose its magnetism quickly.

Electricity (p. 9)
1. a, 2. c, 3. d, 4. b, 5. Coal energy powers a turbine, the turbine runs a generator, the generator turns large copper coils inside huge magnets, producing electricity.

The Milky Way (p. 11)
1. c, 2. d, 3. b, 4. c, 5. A pinwheel with center bulge; three or four spiral arms outward from the center of pinwheel

Animal Kingdom (p. 13)
1. b, 2. c, 3. c, 4. a, 5. Invertebrates do not have backbones; vertebrates have backbones.

Child Labor in Early Textile Mills (p. 15)
1. a, 2. c, 3. d, 4. b, 5. Lint caused lung diseases; machines were dangerous to operate.

Children on the Oregon Trail (p. 17)
1. d, 2. c, 3. c, 4. d, 5. Wagons were packed with supplies so there wasn't much room; to lighten the load, children had to walk.

Leif the Lucky (p. 19)
1. b, 2. d, 3. c, 4. b, 5. Rescued shipwrecked crew; discovered Vinland

Education of Children in Ancient Athens (p. 21)
1. b, 2. a, 3. a, 4. b, 5. To be a knowledgeable leader, responsible citizen, and a skilled soldier

Victory Gardens (p. 23)
1. c, 2. c, 3. a, 4. b, 5. To help the war effort; food was rationed by the government

The Leaders of the Lewis and Clark Expedition (p. 25)
1. b, 2. a, 3. d, 4. b, 5. Served in the military; captains; good woodsmen; co-leaders of the expedition

Rain Forest (p. 27)
1. a, 2. d, 3. b, 4. c, 5. Form a canopy; block out the sunlight; few plants can grow on forest floor; plants adapt and grow up high in the trees where they can receive sunlight; safe place for animals to live

Rivers (p. 29)
1. a, 2. c, 3. d, 4. a, 5. Source of food; fertile land; source of clean water for drinking and cooking

Plate Tectonics (p. 31)
1. c, 2. d, 3. a, 4. d, 5. The supercontinent Pangaea broke apart and formed continents; the continents slowly drifted to present positions.

Geography of the Thirteen Original Colonies (p. 33)
1. c, 2. a, 3. a, 4. b, 5. The warm climate and rich soil produced wheat and other grains.

Geography of the United States (p. 35)
1. a, 2. b, 3. b, 4. d, 5. Source of water; shipping goods; dams for electricity

Ocean Currents and the Fishing Industry (p. 37)
1. c, 2. a, 3. a, 4. a, 5. Answers will vary but must be supported with details from the selection.

Bartering (p. 39)
1. a, 2. d, 3. c, 4. d, 5. Trade goods for services or use online bartering websites; saves money and time

Goods and Services (p. 41)
1. d, 2. b, 3. c, 4. b, 5. Goods are items that we use. Services are any actions that one person or group does for another.

Banking (p. 43)
1. c, 2. a, 3. d, 4. b, 5. Stock market crashed; banks failed; to stop people from changing bank deposits into gold or cash; give banks time to recover

Income Tax (p. 45)
1. b, 2. c, 3. a, 4. a, 5. Shows money earned and tax being withheld; record for employee; shows earnings and deductions

Trade-offs and Opportunity Cost (p. 47)
1. a, 2. a, 3. b, 4. a, 5. Make a list of criteria needed to make decision, list all possible choices, consider pros and cons of each, rank choices, make choice, and identify opportunity cost of the decision.

Needs and Wants (p. 49)
1. b, 2. d, 3. c, 4. b, 5. Needs are necessities. Wants are luxuries.

George Washington Carver (p. 51)
1. c, 2. b, 3. c, 4. b, 5. Answers will vary but might include it provides facts and information at a glance; shows key events as they occurred in Caver's life.

Time Zones (p. 53)
1. d, 2. c, 3. a, 4. a, 5. Answers will vary but might include it helps the reader identify, locate, and compare time in different parts of the United States.

Making Bones Bend (p.55)
1. b, 2. c, 3. a, 4. b, 5. Answers will vary but might include minerals are removed from the bone; vinegar removes the calcium from the bone.

Conestoga Wagons (p. 57)
1. b, 2. d, 3. c, 4. a, 5. Designed to haul freight; sturdy; well-built

School Uniforms (p. 59)
1. a, 2. b, 3. d, 4. a, 5. Answers will vary but must be supported with details from the selection.

Nonfiction Reading Comprehension
Grades 5-6 Standards Matrix

Reading Selections	Content Standards*											
	1	2	3	4	5	6	7	8	9	10	11	12
Science												
Earthquakes	X		X	X	X	X						
Amphibians	X		X	X	X	X						
Magnets	X		X	X	X	X						
Electricity	X		X	X	X	X						
The Milky Way	X		X	X	X	X						
Animal Kingdom	X		X	X	X	X						
History												
Child Labor in Early Textile Mills	X		X	X	X	X						
Children on the Oregon Trail	X		X	X	X	X						
Leif the Lucky	X		X	X	X	X						
Education of Children in Ancient Athens	X		X	X	X	X						
Victory Gardens	X		X	X	X	X						
Leaders of the Lewis and Clark Expedition	X		X	X	X	X						
Geography												
Rain Forest	X		X	X	X	X						
Rivers	X		X	X	X	X						
Plate Tectonics	X		X	X	X	X						
Geography of the Thirteen Original Colonies	X		X	X	X	X						
Geography of the United States	X		X	X	X	X						
Ocean Currents and the Fishing Industry	X		X	X	X	X						
Economics												
Bartering	X		X	X	X	X						
Goods and Services	X		X	X	X	X						
Banking	X		X	X	X	X						
Income Tax	X		X	X	X	X						
Trade-offs and Opportunity Cost	X		X	X	X	X						
Needs and Wants	X		X	X	X	X						
Informational Text												
George Washington Carver (Timeline)	X		X	X	X	X						
Time Zones (Map)	X		X	X	X	X						
Making Bones Bend (Science Experiment)	X		X	X	X	X						
Field Trip Request (Letter)	X		X	X	X	X						
Conestoga Wagons (Diagram)	X		X	X	X	X						
School Uniforms (Editorials)	X		X	X	X	X						

*The content standards are the IRA/NCTE Standards for the English Language Arts. For a brief description of the standards, go to <http://www.ncte.org/standards>. For more detailed information on each content standard, see the book *Standards for the English Language Arts* (ISBN 0-8141-4676-7).

Photo Credits

pg. 1 Elementary school classroom ©iStockphoto.com/monkeybusiness images

pg. 2 Kinemetrics seismograph {{GNU}} Kkkdc. 25 Aug. 2006. <http://commons.wikimedia.org/wiki/File:Kinemetrics_seismograph.jpg>

pg. 2 Vespucio Norte Highway after 2010 earthquake {{CC}} Esteban Maldonado, Santiago, Chile. 1 Mar. 2010. <http://www.flickr.com/people/38631801@NO7>

pg. 4 Frogspawn closeup {{GNU}} Tarquin. 23 Mar. 2004. <http://en.wikipedia.org>

pg. 4 Tadpoles 10 days {{GNU}} Tarquin. 3 Apr. 2004. <http://en.wikipedia.org>

pg. 4 Frog-Zhe {{PD-USGOV-FWS}} Fanghong. 27 May 2005. <http://longlake.fws.gov/Photo%20Albums/Research%20Album/>

pg. 4 Micrixalus {{GNU}} L. Shyamal, Wynaad. 2006. <http://www.commons.wikimedia.org/wiki/File:Micrixalus.jpg>

pg. 6 Bar magnet {{GFDL}} Aney. 12 Mar. 2006. <http://commons.wikimedia.org/wiki/File:Bar_magnet.jpg>

pg. 8 Francis Turbine complete {{GNU}} Stahlkocher. 28 Mar. 2004. Kaboldy. <http://commons.wikimedia.org/wiki/File:Francis_Trubine_complete.jpg>

pg. 10 Milky Way IR Spitzer {{PD-US GOV-NASA}} NASA/JPL-Caltech/S. Stolovy (SSC/Caltech). 10 Jan. 2006. <http:www.spitzer.caltech.edu/Media/releases/ssc2006-02/ssc2006-02a.shtml>

pg. 10 Milky Way 2005 {{PD-USGOV-NASA}} NASA/JPL-Caltech/R. Hurt. 3 Jun. 2008. <http://www.nasa.gov/mission_pages/spitzer/multimedia/20080603a.html>

pg. 12 Regenwurm1 {{GNU}} Michael Linnenbach. 16 Feb. 2005 <http://commons.wikimedia.org/wiki/File:Regenwurm1.jpg>

pg. 12 Baby elephants3 {{GFDL-WITH-DISCALIMERS}} Sandra Fenley 22 Nov. 2008. Closedmouth. <http://en.wikipedia.org/wiki/File:Baby_elephants3.jpg>

pg. 14 SlaterMill {{GNU}} Forest J. Handford. 23 Sept. 2006 <http://en.wikipedia.org/wiki/File:SlaterMill.jpg

pg. 14 AddieCard05282vLewisHine {{PD-Old/LOC}} E.F. Brown/Lewis Hine. Feb. 1910. Library of Congress, Prints & Photographs Division, National Child Labor Committee Collection, Reproduction Number: LC-DIG-nclc-01830 <http://hdl.loc.gov/loc.pnp/nclc.05282>

pg. 16 Homesteader NE 1866 {{PD-Old}} NARA-ARC Identifier 518267. 1886. <http://en.wikipedia.org/wiki/File:Homesteader_NE_1866.png

pg. 18 Seattle's Leif Erikson statue {{CC}} Steven Pavlov. 4 Apr. 2009. <http://commons.wikimedia.org/wiki/File:Seattle's_Leif_Erikson_statue.jpg

pg. 20 Athena Parthenos Altemps Inv8622 {{PD-Art}} Antiochos, copy of Phidias. 1st century B.C. Photo by Marie-Lan Nguyen. Sept. 2006. Accession number: Inv. 8622 <http://archeoroma.beniculturali.it/museo-nazionale-romano-palazzo-altemps>

pg. 22 "YOUR VICTORY GARDEN COUNTS MORE THAN EVER" - NARA - 516284 {{PD-USGOV}} Office for Emergency Management. Office of War Information. U.S. National Archives and Records Administration. World War II Posters, compiled 1942–1945 (ARC identifier: 513498. <http://arcweb.archives.gov/arc/action/ExternalIdSearch?id=513498>

pg. 22 Victory Gardens. Professor Harry Nelson of San Fransico [sic] gives his daughter and her Girl Scout friends some pointers…-NARA-196479 {PD-USGOV}} Office for Emergency Management. Office of War Information. ca. Feb. 1943. Franklin D. Roosevelt Library. NARA. <http://arcweb.archives.gov/arc/action/ExternalPersonIdSearch?id=1138532>

pg. 26 LTM panorama {{GNU}} T.R. Shankar Raman. 16 Jul. 2008 <http://commons.wikimedia.org/wiki/File:LTM_panorama.jpg>

pg. 28 Dnestr {{GNU}} La luna negra. 18 Mar. 2007. <http://commons.wikimedia.org/wiki/File:Dnestr.jpg>

pg. 30 Pangaea continents {{GNU}} Kieff. 20 Oct. 2009. <http://commons.wikimedia.org/wiki/File:Pangaea_continents.svg>

pg. 36 Krabbenkutter Ivonne Pellworm P5242390jm {{CC-BY-SA-2.0_DE}} Jom. 29 May 2004. <http://en.wikipedia.org/wiki/File:Krabbenkutter_Ivonne_Pellworm_P5242390jm.JPG>

pg. 38 Treaty of Penn with Indians by Benjamin West {{PD-Art}} Benjamin West. 1771–72. Nonenmac. 27 May 2006. <http://en.wikipedia.org/wiki/File:Treaty_of_Penn_with_Indians_by_Benjamin_West.jpg>

pg. 40 Baker infront of oven ©iStockphoto.com/Joas

pg. 42 Westpac ATM {{CC-BY-SA-2.5}} Andrew Garrett. 21 Oct. 2006. <http://commons.wikimedia.org/wiki/File:Westpac_ATM.jpg>

pg. 44 Form 1040EZ, 2005 {{PD-USGOV-IRS}} U.S. Internal Revenue Service. 2005. <http://www.irs.gov>

pg. 44 Form W-2, 2006 {{PD-USGOV-IRS}} U.S. Internal Revenue Service. 2006. <http://www.irs.gov>

pg. 46 BackSmithGrind {{PD-Author}} Vlwisconsin. 29 Dec. 2010. <http://en.wikipedia.org/wiki/File:BackSmithGrind.jpg>

pg. 48 Ribeye Steak ©iStockphoto.com/perkmeup

pg. 50 George Washington Carver {{PD-Old-LOC}} 1906. U.S. Library of Congress Prints and Photographs division, digital ID ppmsc.03252 <http://hdl.loc.gov/loc.pnp/ppmsc.03252>

pg. 54 Vinegar, chicken bone, jar ©Jeff Brodsky, Weird Science Kids 714-287-6220 <www.weirdsciencekids.com>

pg. 58 Kennet uniform {{PD-CC-BY-2.5/GNU}} Robertvan1. 4 May 2007. <http://commons.wikimedia.org/wiki/File:Kennet_uniform.jpg>